THE Silent Transformation

How Churches
have experienced the
Power of the NCD
Growth Forces

80 Stories

from all over the world showing
Natural Church Development in action

Christoph Schalk
with Julie Belding and Daniel Catalano

ChurchSmart
RESOURCES
St. Charles, IL 60174
1-800-253-4276

ChurchSmart
RESOURCES

Published by ChurchSmart Resources

We are an evangelical Christian publisher committed to producing excellent products at affordable prices to help church leaders accomplish effective ministry in the areas of Church planting, Church growth, Church renewal and Leadership development.

For a free catalog of our resources call 1-800-253-4276.
Visit us at: *www.churchsmart.com*

Cover design by: Julie Becker

ISBN#: 1-889638-57-9

THE Silent Transformation

Table of Contents

The Growth Forces

We have a little garden in front of our home, and I'm responsible for doing the work in it. As we all know, spring and fall are the seasons when most of the work needs to be done in a garden. But they are also the main seasons for seminars – and these involve me in a lot of traveling. That's why the garden has been a challenge for me: there's much to do at a time when I'm not home!

So one day I went to a bookstore to look for a manual that could help me with my task. There I discovered a book called *Lazy Gardening* — just what I needed! I bought the book and tried to apply it as the author instructed, only to discover that even lazy gardening is a lot of work, especially if you are abroad.

I guess I'd been dreaming, unrealistically, that the whole garden could be cultivated "all by itself." But that was not what happened.

In the New Testament we find a story that seems similar at first glance:

"The kingdom of God is like a man who casts seed upon the ground; and goes to bed at night and gets up by day, and the seed sprouts up and grows — how, he himself does not know. The earth produces crops all by itself; first the blade, then the head, and then the mature grain in the head. But when the crop permits, he immediately puts in the sickle, because the harvest has come." (Mark 4:26-29)

Isn't this about a lazy farmer? About sleeping? Apparently the farmer in this parable merely casts seed upon the ground and then goes to bed. The earth produces crops all by itself. It's almost as if this farmer read *Lazy Farming* and got it to work!

My father's family comes from a farm, and as a child I spent many school holidays there. I always enjoyed helping my grandma and aunt feed the cows as well as working in the fields. For me it was fun, but, as I realized, for them it was hard work. That's how I know that the farmer in this parable of Jesus was not a lazy man. He had to work hard to ensure the earth produced crops "all by itself." He had to prepare the soil, remove the stones, weed, water, fertilize, deal with insects and so on.

And remember this story came from Israel. If you have ever been to Israel, you'll know it's a dry land where no tree grows without an adjacent irrigation pipeline. At the time of Jesus such pipelines did not exist, and watering a whole field was hard work!

But there it is. We read that the earth produces crops "all by itself." What does it mean? As I understand it, this is a great joint venture between God and mankind. While we might think this story makes no mention of God, the Jewish listeners knew God was at work in the expression "all by itself" — because they had a theistic worldview.

In other words, God is the only one responsible for growth, but the farmer is responsible for preparing an environment in which this growth can happen. If the farmer had not prepared the soil and seed, nothing would have happened. On the one hand we know that "God gives the growth" (1 Cor 3:7), but it is also true that we are God's co-workers (1 Cor 3:9). Isn't that fascinating! God wants us to be his co-workers, and he has even given us a job description. Our task is to care for the environment in which he gives the growth. (That's his job description.)

If we want to see our churches grow in a healthy way, we will have to focus on the quality of the soil, not on the quantity of the plants. If we tug at the plants to make them grow faster, we may end up destroying them. Certainly we will never rush the speed of their growth.

The Silent Transformation at Work

This parable and our interpretation of it is not mere theory – more than 40,000 churches from 70 countries have been using Natural Church Development (NCD) (as of the end of 2005) and show, on average, an increased annual growth rate of 51 percent after only 31 months of implementing NCD. The quality of these churches has increased remarkably, and as a consequence they have grown stronger.

Often the stories of these churches are unspectacular, even though the results are. That is why we call it the "silent transformation." Churches are being transformed as they invest in quality and do their part in this divine joint venture while God does his part.

Focusing on the quality of our churches does mean using the right tools and principles. Suppose a medical doctor grew tired of his job and became a farmer. But suppose he continued to use all the principles he had learned in his former profession, even disinfecting his dung fork because he used to clean his surgical instruments this way. How ridiculous that would be!

So how can we become part of this silent transformation? What principles must we use in order to see our churches grow in a healthy way? We call them the growth forces (or "biotic principles" in some older books.) While the growth forces have been covered systematically in other books on Natural Church Development (e.g., *Color Your World With Natural Church Development* by Christian A. Schwarz, *The Implementation Guide to Natural Church Development* by Christian A. Schwarz and Christoph Schalk, or downloadable documents on www.ncdnet.org), this book shares stories of churches from all over the world. What did they experience when they applied the growth forces? Where did they see their churches grow in quality and quantity — all by themselves? How did they take part in the silent transformation?

While the names of the growth forces are somewhat abstract, you will find the stories in this book will bring life to the principles. Here are the six growth forces:

- Interdependence
- Multiplication
- Energy Transformation
- Sustainability (formerly: Multi-usage)
- Symbiosis
- Fruitfulness (formerly: Functionality)

Releasing the "All By Itself" Potential

What is the secret of these principles? How do they make a difference? I had an eye-opening experience when I did an NCD seminar in Bogotá, Colombia, a couple of years ago. There, for the first time in my life, I saw banana plants with ripe bananas on them (outside a botanical garden, of course.) And I was reminded of a special gift I received from my uncle when I was ten years old: a little plastic greenhouse with banana seeds. Banana seeds are pretty big, and it takes a few weeks to see them germinate. However, once it happens they grow very fast, and soon I had to repot the plants from the greenhouse and put them in big containers on our balcony. It was summertime in Germany — and not a problem for these subtropical plants. When the winter drew near, my challenge was to find a warm place for the banana trees, but since they were too big to bring indoors, I had to make a decision.

I decided — as ten-year-old boys do — that these banana plants would be the first ones ever to survive a German winter. Of course, they did not.

Years later in Colombia, I realized the difference between my banana plants and the fruitful plants there. It was not the seeds. The plants could have come from the same seeds. The difference was the environment.

The same is true for our churches: God has given all the potential for growth to our churches (as he does for every little seed.) It is not his fault if our churches do not develop in a healthy way and do not grow. It is our responsibility — as God's co-workers — to create an environment where our churches *can* grow. And it is the growth forces that release the God-given growth potential and make the difference.

In the following chapters you will find 80 stories from countries on all continents — a whole bunch of learning experiences on how to apply the growth forces. Discover what others in your own or in other cultures have discovered, and individualize these principles for your own church. Learn to think church according to the growth forces, learn to be and to live as church according to the growth forces, and learn to lead your church by these same principles. Then you too will experience the silent transformation in your congregation. May this book inspire you to be part of God's work.

How You Will Benefit Most From This Book

This book can be used in different settings — for example for personal reading and reflection, for small group discussion, for training co-workers in biotic thinking, and for strengthening the growth forces during an NCD process.

The stories of this book have been categorized according to the six growth forces. However, most stories refer to more than just one force, and some of them to all six. Thus the categorization is somewhat subjective and only serves the purpose of helping find a starting point to identify the growth forces.

While this book shares stories of people and churches from all over the world, it does not repeat all the theoretical background of the growth forces that has been published elsewhere. We highly recommend that you read *Color Your World with Natural Church Development* along with this book to find answers to such questions as:

- What is our definition of a "principle"?
- What are *universal* principles?
- What is the scientific background of the growth forces?
- What is the biblical background of the growth forces?
- How do the growth forces relate to other elements of Natural Church Development?

By the way: Finding these stories in our book does not mean that we recommend you duplicate the methods. This book is intended to help you to *understand* the growth forces more deeply, not to *copy* from others.

Personal Reflection

Every story starts with a short introduction or quote, and ends with a comment and a question for further reflection. You could simply read this book as any other book, and take some time to reflect on the questions after each story. This will help you to gain a deeper understanding of how to apply the growth forces in various situations.

Small Group Discussion

The reflection questions are also good for discussion in small groups. Why not select a few stories (maybe even for a series of small group meetings) and discuss these questions? This will help your whole group to get familiar with the growth forces and learn to apply them in their own lives — and in their ministries.

For each of the growth forces, we have chosen one story and analyzed it in-depth. You will find this systematic growth force analysis at the end of each chapter. If you want to dig deeper in your small group, you may want to read and discuss these showcase studies.

Another approach for your group could be to use the growth force checklist that you will find in the appendix (page 145) as an outline for the group discussion. In this case, you should discuss only one or two stories in a meeting.

Biotic Training

Being aware of the growth forces leads to healthy church life and healthy leadership decisions. Without this awareness we risk doing church in an unbalanced or biased way, becoming either technocratic or spiritualistic. That is why it is important to think biotically (biotic = life-giving).

If you want to train co-workers, leaders and members of your church to think and act according to the growth forces, use the growth force checklist and selected stories for discussion — just as you might do in any small group. In addition, you could use the systematic analyses at the end of each chapter as examples.

NCD Process

If your church is going through an NCD cycle as part of the NCD process, this book could be used for all the purposes mentioned above, and to train the implementation team. It could be used to share "biotic examples" in sermons, demonstrate the fruit and the outcomes of the NCD process, motivate and train members and leaders, and support biotic/(life-giving) thinking in all kinds of ministries and groups of your church. This book, then, is a must-read for spreading this new paradigm into all parts of the church.

GROWTH FORCE 1:

INTERDEPENDENCE

Interdependence refers to the church as the Body of Christ: a body with many parts, in which all parts are connected and interdependent. Paul says: "If one part suffers, every part suffers with it." (1 Cor 12:26). It is often a challenge to understand all the relationships within the church. If you want to understand the human body, perhaps because you want to become a medical doctor, it takes years of learning. But the Body of Christ is more complex. Simple, linear cause-and-effect thinking does not work. It is our job to get a deeper and deeper understanding of the church and how its different parts are connected, and to anticipate the long-term consequences of our decisions.

STORY 1 — USA: "BUT THE MINISTRY'S MY BABY!"

"The way to healthy interdependence is to be able to see things clearly — to see people, situations, life dynamics and most of all ourselves clearly. If we are not working on healing our childhood wounds and changing our childhood programming then we cannot begin to see ourselves clearly let alone anything else in life." — Robert Burney

In my twenties I was beginning my career and marriage and having children. But having grown up in a dysfunctional family, with many tough questions to work through, I wondered how I was going to lead my own family. I had much to learn about *control* and *relationships* and God answered my questions. That period in which I was getting my private world in order and spending little time in public ministry was what I now call my "cocoon years."

In my thirties I began a public ministry, working with children. That first year was overwhelming, but by the end of it I was beginning to get my sea legs. Then I started asking myself key questions, as I had done in my twenties.

What *was* a healthy team? And having come from dysfunction myself, how did I *start* such a team?

This search led me to NCD principles. I probably applied these naturally in many situations, but it was good to have some research and something objective to refer to.

As I studied these helpful principles it seemed to me *interdependence* was the most powerful one of all. The *Implementation Guide* talks about a "Cobra Effect" — the tendency we all have to go for quick results without understanding the long-term consequences.

The study had a powerful effect on my life and ministry. For starters, I now carry a lighter load. Since I continue to oversee about 300 adult volunteers who work with children, how is that possible?

Think about becoming a new parent. We all try so hard at first, don't we? At some point, if we didn't go through a process of release we'd never sleep at night. For the first few weeks we tend to check the baby constantly to see if he's still breathing. After a while we stop doing this and relax. We tell ourselves we're doing our best and must let some things go.

It's the same with ministry. We worry about it because it's our baby, and having invested in it we naturally want to see it go well. But if we're not careful the anxiety can zap the joy right out of us.

Early in my ministry I'd fret over every negative piece of feedback, every decision. As a result I'd come home to my family exhausted, and it wasn't much joy for them either.

Over time I began to look at what I'd learned as a parent, and realized I had to release the control of my ministry — my new baby — to God.

The result? Well, the emotional and physical demands are still there and I still get tired. But God has gradually changed me. As a leader I now — thankfully — carry much less stress. This has freed me up to enjoy my days off, my wife, my children and yes, even my chaotic weekend ministry! [*interdependence*]

But there's been a bonus: having now been released myself, I've learned to release others to God.

Edmond, one of my leaders, was struggling, and he confessed to me his marriage was rocky. He also told me he was concerned about his own eleven-year-old son who was becoming increasingly withdrawn.

I knew my team at work started with the adults that led the kids, and not the kids themselves.

And so I had my famous "balance" talk with Edmond, as I've since had with several other volunteers when I've felt the Spirit prompt me.

"I know you want to fulfill your role as a volunteer and to serve the children that are in your care," I told him. "But as leader I have to look at the 5-10-20 year history of our church. I have to be able to look back on these years and know that I cared for every child, including those in your family. I have to trust that if we need to let you rest or go to counseling, or make time for your spouse or children, that's okay. I have to trust that as you get your private world in order, God will somehow protect the public aspect of our ministry."

He was overwhelmed. He also took the time out that I suggested, to spend more time with his family.

God really is in charge. And the trust factor in my department has rocketed.

"Never have I felt cared for by a leader at a church like I have with you," one volunteer wrote on a card. "I know you are thinking of my family and for that I am thankful."

Wow! Trust is the first of many things you will observe as you release the principle of interdependence in yourself and your teams. You'll also see increased efficiency and effectiveness. It's a sort of "anti-Cobra Effect." As we release the short-term concerns and think long term, the short term seems less urgent.

The bottom line is that things will stay balanced if we don't meddle with God's natural design. People are designed to enjoy him. Nothing should get in the way of that. Not even serving at church!

St Augustine (354-430 A.D.) once said, "Trust the past to God's mercy, the present to God's love and the future to God's providence."

For reflection/discussion: *Why do we find it so hard to leave our ministry in the hands of God?*

STORY 2 — RUSSIA: WE NEED EACH OTHER

God wired all of us in such a way that we can only fulfill his purposes for our lives in community, in his family, and in relationship with one another.

Chapter Twelve of First Corinthians has always fascinated — and frightened — me as it speaks of the church and its members. It encourages me by reminding me that I'm not alone and that my ministry matters. It also encourages relationships, as we understand how valuable we are individually, but realize at the same time that we cannot live without others.

I like organizing camps but it's a complicated task that requires many helpers. Our church is quite small (less than thirty members) and usually half of us are involved in arranging these camps: some members are responsible for clean-up, some for food, some for activities, others for worship or for leading small groups. But we are all united by a common goal — to create a good camp where families or friends can enjoy this time with one another. [*interdependence*]

As I mentioned before, there's also something in that chapter that frightens me. Verse 26 says, "If one part suffers, every part suffers with it..." So if one member has problems, everybody is affected.

Suppose the person who is responsible for the food says to us, "I'm sorry but I'm not up to it this time." What happens then? Do we cancel everything? Do we continue? How will it affect the program of the camp?

Can just one person affect the outcome of the whole event? Yes he can, if he tells himself, "Well, I really don't matter all that much!"

In fact each and every person is important to God, and what we do has a significant effect on everything that happens.

Similarly I'm mindful of how my decisions can change my relationship with others, and how they can affect the fulfillment of our mission. So I remember the proverb — *Measure thrice and cut once*. Yes, we are all parts of one body, we're all dependent on one another, and we are all moving towards the same goal.

Of course there will be obstacles and temptations that affect individuals. But if we encourage one another in times of trouble, we'll be a blessing to those around us and God will get the glory.

> *"Dreams pass into the reality of action. From the actions stems the dream again; and this interdependence produces the highest form of living." — Anais Nin, novelist, 1903-1977*
>
> ***For reflection/discussion:*** *How do you personally understand the proverb, "Measure thrice and cut once"?*

STORY 3 — ROMANIA: UNITY IN DIVERSITY

The church of Jesus Christ is a complex organism with many parts that are inter-related according to God's plan. Explaining this in his first letter to the Corinthians, the Apostle Paul wrote: "I want you to think about how all this makes you more significant, not less. A body isn't just a single part blown up into something huge. It's all the different-but-similar parts arranged and functioning together." 1 Corinthians 12:14 (The Message)

The small church I belong to in Hunedoara is only three years old, but I can already see the growth forces at work in our activities, enabling us to become more productive.

I can vouch for the importance of interdependence. Each of us who is involved in a ministry of the church comes from a different background.

Johann has a degree from a Bible seminary. Andreas never went to high school. We all have different levels of education and theological training, but we understand the importance of team work, and in a spirit of humility we accept our diversity and use it to our advantage.

In fact we appreciate the variety! Maybe it's a reaction to the dull uniformity the communists imposed on us for so many years. Since we realize our gifts are complementary, there is no need for competition within the church.

"One of the great miracles of God's creation is the interdependence of its parts from the minutest micro-organisms to the most magnificent stars. Our minds can hardly grasp the wisdom of this self-regulating system of inter-related elements." — Christian Schwarz, author of ***Natural Church Development****.*

For reflection/discussion: *Are there ever circumstances where competition within the church may be appropriate?*

STORY 4 — AUSTRALIA: SERVING OUT OF PASSION RATHER THAN DUTY

So often our best efforts are less than fruitful because the workers we engage for a particular task are not gifted for it. This church realized the hard way that trying to fit square pegs into round holes doesn't work.

Within our church's local community we realized that parents with young children needed an opportunity to socialize.

"Why don't we set up a weekly playgroup?" someone suggested brightly. "Then parents with young children could meet together and talk about their concerns and gain all kinds of new friends. We could invite some of these parents to come to our worship services and small groups and some of them might become followers of Jesus!"

So we set up a playgroup. Sue took on the leadership somewhat reluctantly, because the need was there and she was available, but she had had little experience in children's work.

In hindsight we overlooked an important factor when we appointed the leader. We really needed someone who was gifted with children and passionate about them [*interdependence*] and at that time our church lacked such a person.

This did not stop the playgroup from growing, however. In fact it was so popular that we added a second session to accommodate the demand, and more church members were roped in to help.

Over the months, however, the workers in the playgroup who were engaging with both parents and children were becoming increasingly drained. It's true that one person came to the church and discovered the truth of Christ's love and grace. But the reality had to be faced: the group would have no long term future without a passionate person in charge.

At one of our members' meetings, Pete, a church deacon, put it to us directly:

"Could it be," he asked, "that keeping the group going might, in the end, cause a disservice, rather than a service, to the kingdom of God?"

After much discussion we decided to close the playgroup, which meant that those who were serving in this area were now released to minister in areas where they were appropriately gifted and passionate. It seemed like a hard decision, but in the long run it was best for our community of faith.

The best job can become onerous if we are not gifted for it. If there's a job to be done, it's worth waiting for the person who has been prepared by God to do it. Then everyone involved is blessed.

For reflection/discussion: *Is there anything else this church might have done with the playgroup besides closing it?*

STORY 5 — NORWAY: FINDING A WAY TO BE USEFUL

The desire to feel useful is a universal human need, and the heart is happiest when it beats for others. This church found a way to help its estranged members feel more valuable both to their church and to their community.

In 2002, when the local community board held its quarterly meeting, the community chest had almost run dry.

"I'm sorry," said the city manager, "but in order to meet our budget, some current programs will have to be axed — including the 'Evergreens.'"

Our congregation was appalled. We all knew how much the senior citizens in the community enjoyed their monthly get-together. This program, called 'The Evergreens,' had been run for years by the town council.

"I have an idea," said Erika, when the problem was being discussed at a church meeting. "Why couldn't our church take over the running of the Evergreens?"

The idea gathered momentum, and soon it was decided: from now on we would run the program ourselves, on the first Thursday of every month.

Ingrid, a woman from the congregation, was appointed to manage it. Rarely had a lay person headed up any of our church ministries before. Until then, most of them had been led by members of the pastoral staff.

Some women agreed to go on the roster for making coffee, while others took turns in preparing the refreshments.

"What shall we do with the money we collect?" Anna asked.

"Let's give it to the church," someone else suggested, "to cover the kitchen costs."

There have been other benefits. Most of the women taking their turn in the kitchen to prepare the food were not active in the church. Now there is a new place for them to serve, and our church is showing what gift-based ministry can look like.

"I'd practically dropped out of church," said Kirsten as she poured the coffee one Thursday morning. "I just didn't feel I had anything to contribute. Now that I feel I can do something useful, I've become part of the church again."

> *"Everybody can be great... because anybody can serve. You don't have to have a college degree to serve. You don't have to make your subject and verb agree to serve. You only need a heart full of grace. A soul generated by love." — Martin Luther King, Jr. (1929-1968), American civil rights leader.*
>
> ***For reflection/discussion:*** *What issues prevent churches from using their lay people more fully in community service?*

STORY 6 — RUSSIA: "FAITH WITH SHOE LEATHER"

> ***Gift-based ministry is powerful in its effect. When Christians serve in their area of giftedness, they generally function less in their own strength and more in the power of the Holy Spirit. Thus ordinary people can accomplish the extraordinary! (Christian A. Schwarz)***

There is a group in our fellowship called the Home League. Sixteen to eighteen women meet once a week to knit mittens and socks, to sew, and to embroider. They also learn new songs that we later sing in our Sunday meetings. We sell the things that are made in Home League and use some of the money to support one of the church's ministries, such as the soup kitchen. One lady from the Home League also serves there as a cook.

We invite people who come to the soup kitchen to attend our Sunday meetings. In this way we strengthen the church, because these people later start to come to Bible studies and prayer meetings and move closer to God.

Since we all need one another, how important it is to cultivate our relationships!

"One thing I know; the only ones among you who will be really happy are those who will have sought and found how to serve," said Albert Schweitzer (1875-1965), the German missionary, theologian and philosopher. This circle of Russian women discovered friendship evangelism as they pooled their talents for a common cause.

For reflection/discussion: *Is there a practical ministry your church could initiate to help the poor in your community?*

STORY 7 — LATVIA: ENJOYING THE SYMPHONY

In some ways the church is like an orchestra, with each member playing a different instrument to produce beautiful music. Sometimes, though, the harmony needs to be worked at!

Last summer four of us young people went to Norway. The Sunday after we returned, we knew our pastor would ask us to say something to the church. Being used to leading, I automatically began to plan what I would say.

"I think I'll focus on the Oslo meetings," I said, as we talked over coffee. "After all, they were the most important events in the whole trip. I could do a power point presentation and..."

"Hold on, Ivan!" Anna flashed back, a little heatedly. "I think we should talk about the street witnessing at Skien. As far as I was concerned, that was the highlight of the trip and I think people would be really interested to hear about it."

"I agree," said Natasha. "And I'd also like to share that experience in Stavenger with the church."

"I'd like to talk about the Bergen visit," Maria put in. "That was kind of special for me."

Privately, I felt I could handle the presentation better than anyone.

The others could speak well, but I felt the visits to Stavenger or Bergen hardly merited a mention. In my view it was the Oslo meetings that had really focused us spiritually.

I even felt resentful that others wanted the limelight. Not that I showed it, of course. I simply tried to find out what they wanted to say.

We chose some songs to sing but did not decide on the speaker. Feeling somewhat put out, I asked God for wisdom, peace and patience.

Surprisingly, I felt quite excited when Sunday morning arrived. By this time my attitude had changed completely, and rather than wanting to speak, I was content to lead the singing.

I observed a real passion in the hearts of the girls to share what God had done, while I threw my heart into the praise and worship. What they had to say was just what the congregation needed to hear at that moment, and we all felt God's blessing and peace.

[*interdependence*]

As I look back I realize everyone needs to use their spiritual gifts. If more than one person has the same gift, then we need to look to God who will direct us for the encouragement of all.

In a church that functions well there are no prima donnas. Each member must be sensitive to the needs of the others so that all can use their gifts for the good of the whole.

For reflection/discussion: *Can you think of another situation where the use of spiritual gifts in a church could cause a problem? What principles should leaders follow in order to preserve unity within the congregation?*

STORY 8 — USA: NO COMPETITION HERE

The Apostle Paul wrote: "If you've gotten anything at all out of following Christ, if his love has made any difference in your life, if being in a community of the Spirit means anything to you, if you have a heart, if you care — then do me a favour: Agree with each other, love each other, be deep-spirited friends... Put yourself aside and help others get ahead. Don't be obsessed with getting your own advantage. Forget yourselves long enough to lend a helping hand." (Philippians 2:10-4, The Message)

In 1978 I came to Jefferson to be the pastor at Sunnyside, an independent charismatic church. Jefferson at the time was much like any other small American town with its various churches barely aware of one another.

But an amazing thing started to happen in 1988, after I had a call from Bob Simes, the Baptist pastor.

"Eric," he said, "I've just been to a denominational prayer summit, and through it all I've felt God speaking to me about praying for the other churches in the city. How do you feel about this?"

"I'll give it some thought," I said.

Normally I wouldn't have been interested. Looking after my own church took up more than enough of my time, and I hardly needed another commitment. But for the last few months I'd been challenged by the Holy Spirit regarding my denominational pride and isolationism.

And I realized that although both Bob and I had been pastoring in the same town for more than ten years, we hardly knew each other. The number of times we had talked together could have been counted on both hands.

"Thanks," said Bob. "We're starting a monthly prayer meeting here, on the first Friday, just to pray for God's blessing on the other churches in Jefferson. Come along if you're free and want to."

He gave me details and I was convicted. How could I refuse to even try it?

So I went. And the next month I went again, and kept on going. I found myself actually enjoying getting to know the other pastors — even the ones whose traditions differed widely from my own. Where once I'd almost prided myself on our independence as a church, I actually began to relish these new relationships.

We pastors began to attend prayer summits together and to co-sponsor the community Good Friday service. Our churches began to co-mingle. Over a period of several years Bob and I went to school together and spent many hours developing a friendship.

One day one of the pastors suggested, "Why don't we begin a leaders' weekly prayer breakfast?"

This took off with enthusiasm. Friendships continued to build and as churches within the town had needs, other churches would see how they could help meet them. Churches sent gifted musicians to lead worship in another church, and when pulpits needed to be filled there was an exchange of personnel. Members of one church were hired for staff positions at another; and children's ministries combined efforts for community events and Sunday school needs. [*interdependence*]

As trust grew, competition between us was no longer an issue. It was replaced by a spirit of brotherhood, family and service, and we pledged to express only positive things about the other churches.

Whenever I met Bob I'd give him a hug and let him know the charismatics were praying for him and the Baptists. He'd do the same thing.

The churches began a summer community service on Main Street and we continued to exchange resources.

As time passed Sunnyside went through a rough patch and a group of disgruntled people quit attending, reducing our number by almost half. The financial burden was overwhelming and I shared the sad story with Bob and the others, as a matter for prayer.

We were overwhelmed when Bob's church took a building fund offering and gave a tithe of it to Sunnyside. This gift of $10,000 increased not only the good will but also the level of commitment of the Christians within each local church to the body of Christ as a whole.

Today we're still strongly committed to encouraging one another. We share staff members, resources and congregations, while each church retains its distinctives. [*interdependence*]

> *"Never forget that it was Christ who, by his passion on the cross, made each one of us acceptable to God. If you are acceptable to*

God, what possible reason could I find to make you unacceptable to me!" — Warren Litzman

For reflection/discussion: *What would it take for the churches in your community to enjoy greater fellowship with one another?*

STORY 9 — LATVIA: EVERYONE CAN LEND A HAND

"Interdependence is and ought to be as much the ideal of man as self-sufficiency. Man is a social being. Without interrelation with society he cannot realize his oneness with the universe or suppress his egotism. His social interdependence enables him to test his faith and to prove himself on the touchstone of reality." — Mahatma Gandhi.

Ten years ago I started my ministry as pastor in Aizpute. At that time the church had about seventy members, but only twenty-five came to the meetings and in the last few months there had been no newcomers. People in the street were just not interested in attending our services.

At that time I had no work experience, nor any clue about NCD. I attempted different strategies — even tried pressuring people — but nothing worked.

"Blow it!" I told myself in frustration one day. "Since the church doesn't appreciate me I'll invest some of my energy elsewhere!"

I still preached on Sundays, of course, but I found other things to do. From time to time I helped to organize civic activities, and I also worked at the local TV channel.

Looking back I am impressed at how wonderfully God led my ministry and the church. Because of my busyness I just didn't have time to manage everything that I (as I thought) needed to do. So out of necessity I asked a few church members to take on some responsibilities. I asked a retired carpenter to chair the building committee and a single woman with musical gifts to organize the opening worship on Sundays. Various other leadership tasks were also delegated.

To my surprise it worked! We all became involved in the work of the ministry, and gradually more people began to attend the meetings [*interdependence*].

Only later, as I read more about church leadership, did I recognize the wrong thinking that had caused a major problem for our congregation. The previous pastor had done everything by himself, and I'd simply followed suit. But our members needed to play a more active part in ministry, and after they began to do so, the number of the people attending our meetings actually doubled within two years!

God taught me through experience what was later confirmed through my studies — that everyone has a role in the ministry of a church.

> *"Let's face it. In most of life we really are interdependent. We need each other. Staunch independence is an illusion, but heavy dependence isn't healthy, either. The only position of long-term strength is interdependence: win/win." (Greg Anderson)*
>
> ***For reflection/discussion:*** *If you are a church leader, what are the main issues that prevent you from delegating more of your responsibilities to others?*

STORY 10 — ROMANIA: KEEPING THE TEAMS IN CONTACT

> ***One of the risks of delegation is to lose sight of the common vision. This Romanian church overcame a potential problem in this regard by scheduling regular meetings of its department heads.***

Our church has been growing since we established clear values and priorities in regard to discipleship, team leadership, power sharing, strategy, vision and mission. As our membership has grown, so has the number of departments within the church. Currently we have eleven departments, some defined by function and others by social groupings. There are departments for children, teenagers, students, young adults, women, seniors, worship, evangelization, mission, pastoral care and administration. As a pastoral team we have delegated authority and responsibility to the department heads who are required to manage a leadership team within each department.

This process ("decentralization") has had some positive spin-offs. The leaders are having a strong impact as they become trained and involved in specialized ministry. And there are many departments in which people can now serve with their specific gifts. Thus our members are being better served and cared for.

There was the risk, however, that we could work so well within our separate departments that we might lose the common vision of the church. To avoid this, the eleven department heads meet monthly in order to foster unity within the church as a whole. Through these meetings we get to know the objectives of each department and its needs, and we schedule activities together [*interdependence*]. It's a good time to evaluate how we are fulfilling our goals as a church and what improvements we need to make, and it creates a sense of interdependence in our work. This is clearly seen in the major events of church life: the baptisms of new converts and the celebration of Easter, the Feast of Tabernacles and Christmas.

Communication works for those who work at it. Usually in our busy lives we have to make time to relate to others — but when we do our effectiveness and productivity invariably increase.

For reflection/discussion: *How well do you know what other leaders in your church are doing?*

STORY 11 — CZECH REPUBLIC: "OF SUCH IS , THE KINGDOM OF HEAVEN."

"The soul is healed by being with children"
— Fyodor Dostoyevsky, Russian novelist, 1821-1881

Children — wherever they are — usually bring joy and laughter, not to mention a bit of mess and noise. God has blessed us with many of these little ones who persistently demand our patience and love. It's a joy but also a responsibility for the adults who must guide them. We are to teach our children to fear the Lord, know his ways and trust him.

Our church wants children to become Christ's disciples and serve him wholeheartedly. So every Sunday our children have been meeting during the worship service to learn more about the Lord.

We are aware, however, that it's not just church children who need guidance. Wherever we went we found children who had never heard about Christ. So we were delighted to be able to reach some of these children through Good News clubs. In this way non-churched youngsters could learn more about God and his love for them.

Thus two different children's ministries developed within our church — one for "Sunday kids" and another for "working day kids." Each had its own goals and staff, and they worked separately.

"What a good idea," you might say, "for a church to provide two different ministries for children!"

True, but there was a problem. On the one hand, we were leading our churched children to become "Sunday Christians," aware they were not rubbing shoulders with other kids and sharing their faith with them. On the other hand, we were not able to bring the Good News Club kids to Sunday School.

One day Hanna, one of the Sunday School leaders, had an idea.

"Why don't we get together with the Good News Club leaders?" she suggested. "There might be some ways we could encourage one another and share some ideas." [*interdependence*].

"I doubt they'd be interested," someone responded. "For one thing, the groups have an entirely different focus."

"Well, we've nothing to lose by talking to them," Hanna insisted. "I'm willing to host a coffee and dessert evening at my home so we can find out if there's any interest in working together."

So it was arranged, and this meeting opened the door to some surprising cooperation.

Both teams slightly adjusted their programs, and now the church benefits from a combined ministry.

"Sunday kids" now meet their Christian friends during the week as well. They play games together and organize various competitions. They also have a place to invite their non-believing friends to, and are learning how to serve.

Non-believing kids from the clubs have started to attend the Sunday School meetings, and are gradually finding out what it means to be a part of a church.

The group leaders are sharing their experiences and adapting the content and form of their meetings, while the children are being provided with useful and relevant programs.

"And you know what?" said Hanna at a recent church meeting when the various departments were presenting their progress reports. "Everyone's growing in the knowledge and love of God!"

Nothing we do for children is ever wasted. This church combined its resources to double the effectiveness of its outreach to young people.

For reflection/discussion: *What could your church do to reach more children from non-churched families?*

STORY 12 — LATVIA: UNITED BY A BUILDING PROJECT

"Using the gift God gave me as a good architect, I designed blueprints; Apollos is putting up the walls. Let each carpenter who comes on the job take care to build on the foundation." (1 Corinthians 3:10 — The Message)

Sometimes it's hard to alter habits or thought patterns. But despite our tendency to cling to old habits, the people in our church are being influenced and changed by the Holy Spirit.

When I started my ministry in Liepaja ten years ago I encountered several needs and problems. A major one was our chronic lack of space, but no one could see a way forward, despite endless discussions.

After five years we had enough money in the building fund to renovate the second part of our church building. This was the catalyst for transformation!

The congregation became fired up as everybody found a way to help [*interdependence, symbiosis*]. Even those who had stood on the sidelines up till then took on small jobs with enthusiasm. As a church we'd never been more united. We had only one desire — to finish the project as soon as possible so we could have a proper place to meet. And we did!

Our ministry with children and youth was then able to expand because we now had separate rooms for each group. But more importantly, we all grew spiritually. The closer we worked together, the better we came to know others and ourselves, and to discover one another's needs, possibilities and character.

"Coming together is a beginning. Keeping together is progress. Working together is success," said Henry Ford (1863-1947) the American industrialist. This church discovered it from experience.

For reflection/discussion: After the project is finished, what steps could this church take to maintain its newfound unity?

STORY 13 — GERMANY: A NETWORK OF MINISTERS

"An individual without information can't take responsibility. An individual with information can't help but take responsibility." — Jan Carlzon.

If a church is to function well, all of its ministers must cooperate. But they first need to know what the others are doing, what drives them, and what works well.

In times past our church elders and the pastor held discrete responsibilities within the church. All three planned the worship and oversaw the Sabbath School. But in addition, David handled the church's administration and took care of public relations; Andreas looked after pastoral and spiritual care, technical services and stewardship; and Franz led the Pathfinder (boy scout) group and was responsible for evangelism, church growth and home groups. Sometimes it almost seemed as if the left hand didn't know what the right hand was doing.

So how could each leader bring others into the loop?

As a church we decided that communications needed to become centralized. Now when someone in our congregation addresses an urgent request to a church elder, it is copied to the other church leaders as well as the pastor. Then the church elder who is responsible for that particular area responds to the request.

This system really works, as we all become aware of outcomes and consequences. For example, information from Pathfinder automatically goes to surrounding churches in our region [*interdependence*].

To clarify mutual expectations within the church, we worked out a description for each ministry. Suddenly everybody was clear about his or her job. Best of all, as we worked through the tasks of each ministry with the people involved, those people took ownership of them. Now when somebody is baffled by a task, he or she simply goes to the head elder with whom they worked on the job description. There is interdependence among church leaders and, if needed, within the whole church.

Almost all the leaders of the various church departments are working with the team that is implementing the NCD process. Thus they are bringing new ideas into all parts of our church life [*interdependence*].

Management guru Stephen R. Covey has written, "Ineffective people live day after day with unused potential. They experience synergy only in small, peripheral ways in their lives. But creative experiences can be produced regularly, consistently, almost daily... It requires enormous personal security and openness and a spirit of adventure."

For reflection/discussion: *Are there any drawbacks to the centralization of communications within a church?*

STORY 14 — CZECH REPUBLIC: REACHING OUT THROUGH MUSICAL DRAMA

The growth force of interdependence states that the way the individual parts are integrated into a whole system is more important than the parts themselves. Here's how a church in the Czech Republic found this to be true.

Our church in the Czech Republic has produced a musical called *Royal Ambassador*, based on the parable of the wedding banquet recorded in Matthew 22:1-10. It is a professional production, lasting about seventy minutes. All the actors are members of our church, aged from four to ninety-nine.

People from the different services of our church have become involved with the musical, which has a team of about sixty. There are Sunday school teachers, youth leaders, teachers from our Christian school, parents of children, choir members, club leaders and other members of our congregation [*symbiosis*].

We wanted this musical to be not only an activity for our church members but also an evangelistic tool. So non-churched people needed to feel at ease with our performance. We also wanted to ensure that those who were taking part in the musical didn't just act and sing about God but also lived out the gospel. Home group leaders served as supervisors of the whole project. This meant each group leader could observe whether the acting members were really willing to share their faith or whether they simply wanted to promote themselves.

This project continues to enhance several areas of church life. The musical itself challenges members of different ministries within the church to use their gifts in various other areas — singing, drama, music, dance, choreography, production, artistic invention, craft, costume design, props, computer skills, animation, sound equipment, children's work, and so on.

But the real goal of the project is to evangelize — in different ways.

More than 4000 members of the general public have already attended the performances. We still can't afford some of the sophisticated equipment, and so we rent this from professionals. These people have already seen the performance several times and some of the actors have become friends with them. When traveling to different places we hire a bus, whose driver is now much more open to the Word of God than he was at first.

The musical is also an excellent event to which people in the church and home groups can invite friends. Individuals learn how to start communicating, and the home groups pray for new friends.

At the end of the program, performers go into the auditorium and share their faith with people in the audience. For many participants this has been a positive experience. Some of them take the challenge seriously and children and youth, especially, have been personally transformed. Many members of our church community have also been challenged to deepen their relationship with God. Working within the musical and going on tour (the last trip was to Slovakia) has strengthened relationships among the church members.

So our musical has encouraged a team of people to work on a new project. But the musical is not the be all and end all of our church life. It's just one mission tool that happens to have provided many opportunities to develop virtues, talents and gifts in our members. We've had to be flexible. Success has come as individuals have become involved and committed, and as they have built relationships and shared common goals. [*interdependence*].

There is strength in numbers, as this church discovered. But more than numbers are involved here. Each part is contributing to the work of the whole. With each member participating in the total effort, the church's primary mission of evangelism has been carried out in a way that has impacted the entire community.

STORY 15 — GERMANY: WORKING FOR A COMMON CAUSE

It has been well said that "Pleasure usually takes the form of ***me*** *and* ***now****; joy is* ***us*** *and* ***always****." (Marvin J. Ashton.) It's also more productive to cooperate than to compete, as the leaders of two ministries with young people discovered.*

As a youth leader, I experienced the power of interdependence and symbiosis a few years ago.

Besides the youth ministry, our church also sponsors another group called Rangers. Both areas had their own infrastructures, which led to certain problems. For example, there was no connection between the two ministries, and much energy was expended on training the workers for each one. There was also some competition between both groups of workers, and the young people noticed this lack of unity. Moreover, some workers from the Rangers attended our youth meetings. While they benefited from our work with young people, they could not fully invest their energies into it because they were busy with the Rangers. Thus we felt somewhat taken advantage of.

After one prayer meeting, the assistant youth leader, Joachim, came up with a suggestion.

"Why don't we set up a combined training program for both groups?" he asked. [*Interdependence*].

"Might work," I said. "I'm willing to give it a try."

So we began to hold training evenings for leaders every two weeks, attended by workers from both the youth ministry and the Rangers. We prayed together, listened to lectures on basic leadership, and had small group discussions. For the next forty-five minutes we then divided into teams to work through everything we had just learned and to decide how to apply it to our ministry.

It was a brilliant move! First, the leaders within both ministries needed to invest less money and effort in preparation because they now worked together and their skills were interchangeable [*interdependence*].

Secondly, the Rangers benefited from the musical talent of Joachim who led the prayer meetings. Thirdly, a growing fellowship developed between the leaders of both groups. As Andreas, the Ranger leader, pointed out, we actually had the same goals.

Fourthly, rather than being competitive, the senior leaders encouraged and praised one another for good lectures and tasks done well.

Joachim was delighted to discover that the junior leaders of the Rangers had benefited spiritually from all the youth meetings and could use what they had learned in their own task of equipping the next generation.

When some leaders left the Rangers ministry to work with the church youth, Andreas admitted he found that difficult.

'But we're all here to serve young people,' he said. "So I need to look at the big picture. I'm grateful that my co-workers are using their skills in a related ministry." [*interdependence*].

"Those who bring sunshine into the lives of others, cannot keep it from themselves." — James M. Barrie.

For reflection/discussion: *Losing workers to another ministry is never easy. If you were the pastor of this church, how would you have encouraged the Rangers leader?*

Growth Force Analysis of this Story:

Isn't this a typical situation in many churches? Two ministries work with the same target group (young people) but have different approaches. Each one is enormously valuable and meets specialized needs, but both ministries run into difficulties. As a leader you can easily apply the principle of interdependence by occasionally asking yourself where the current process might lead, if it continues the way it is going. These leaders showed they were aware of the uncertainties and the competitive atmosphere on both sides, and perceived the negative consequences of this. By taking sensitive heed of this reality, they could start to apply the principle of interdependence. This resulted in positive, long-term change.

The leaders needed to ask themselves how a sense of competition had arisen between their teams, and who was affected by it. What common goals had they overlooked? What common cause could bind them together so they could overcome their present difficulties?

An important key was understanding that both ministries had the goal of teaching and training young youth leaders. While they had always known this, they had never seen the possibility or the urgency of training those leaders together.

By combining the leadership training for the two ministries the directors could maximize their human resources. This resulted in a gain not only of time and strength, but also of space. It also provided a base for fellowship and the exchange of ideas, releasing a new positive atmosphere and motivating all the members of the ministries.

True leaders, like the ones in this story, are not threatened by a diversity of forms, ministries, programs and styles. They don`t favor one group over another but strive to help each one understand how a symbiotic relationship will be beneficial to all. So the principle of *symbiosis* also comes into play, and potentially other growth forces as well.

The more two ministries understand their common goals as well as their individual strengths and tasks, the better the partnership of those ministries. The benefits of this unity then become obvious to *all* members, not just the leaders. No ministry need feel threatened by another, when it knows its specific purpose.

The youth ministry and the Ranger ministry had the common goal of training and equipping young leaders, but each also had its own approach. True symbiosis means valuing different approaches and seeing them as complementary.

GROWTH FORCE 2:

MULTIPLICATION

Nowhere in God's creation can you find unlimited growth. Any entity comes to a point where multiplication is needed. Discipleship is a key strategy for multiplication in the Bible. Up to the present Jesus hasn't been bringing individuals into his Kingdom by himself; instead he invested in a few followers who were sent to disciple all nations by multiplying themselves. Multiplication has a greater growth potential than addition, but it often starts small. In an age when many people are looking for quick fixes and big numbers, addition is the temptation — but it will, in the long run, bring less fruit than multiplication.

STORY 1 — ROMANIA: FROM COMPLAINT TO CELEBRATION

"Why have small groups? So the church can once again become an irresistible Christian community where a person can: love and be loved, know and be known, serve and be served, celebrate and be celebrated." — Rick Diefenderfer

The people in the house group I started were on the pastor's counseling list. But gradually their lives began to improve. The guys were experiencing better marriages [*transformation of energy*] and no longer needed counseling.

"Do you mind if I bring an atheist friend from my work to our next meeting?" a member asked me one day.

"That's fine," I answered. "But why would he want to come with you to a Christian meeting?"

"Well," Joachin answered sheepishly, "I guess he's hearing better stories from me these days. I used to moan a bit about my marriage. But that's sorted out now."

So outsiders started coming to the group, and they began to hear how God was working in their co-workers' lives. This cell has multiplied, and now it's like a magnet for the men's non-Christian friends [*multiplication, sustainability*].

As the men grew closer to the Lord, they sorted out their problems with their families and with each other and now they do need-meeting evangelism for their non-Christian friends who still have marriage difficulties [*interdependence*].

"I know I used to be a real pain in this group," Joachin grinned, "I hope I'm better company now."

"Hey, you're a genuine blessing to the church," I told him, "and to others."

When people feel heard, they feel loved; when they feel loved, they return; and when they return, life transformation happens.

For reflection/discussion: *What might draw secular people to a Christian home group?*

STORY 2 — KENYA: "THE FOUNTAIN OF LIFE"

God is always ready to help us when we ask him. But sometimes we don't realize how willing people are to help us — until we ask them.

The Turkana people are among the poorest and least educated tribes of Kenya. Contact with Western missionaries has been rare, and since the Turkanas are nomadic herders, it has been hard to establish churches among them. Add to this an uninviting climate in which temperatures can soar above 100 degrees F.

In 1998, after we had established the Fountain of Life churches in Kenya (of which there are now more than 80 congregations), a young man from Turkana (a province in Kenya's northwest) approached me.

"I wish you would plant some churches among my people!" he said.

"Well, we could do that," I said cautiously, "but who would look after all these new churches?"

"I will!" he said. "I've just graduated from Bible School in Nairobi!"

So three of us set out to visit Turkana.

When we reached the parched region I discovered an unfamiliar sight. All along the road were little semi-naked boys and girls. In fact some of the boys were stark naked! They waved at us, evidently wanting something. But how much food, I wondered, would it take to feed them all?

For many hours we drove along a rough road, often slowing to a snail pace because of the huge pot holes. The vegetation which had been a deep green at our point of departure was now just grey and brown brush. It was not the Kenya I'd known all my life.

Traveling north towards Lodwar, we stopped to eat lunch under one of the trees. The only creatures we saw were the tiny dik-diks, a few rabbits and lizards. The trip seemed endless, and in the encroaching darkness nothing was familiar.

When we stopped in one of the Turkana villages, naked children came up to us again.

"What do you want?" I asked them.

"A bottle of water, please sir," they replied.

"Is that all?"

"Yes!"

We realized it had been hours since we'd seen any river, or even a spring. But we had brought just enough water for our small team and hadn't a hope of helping all these thirsty children.

We later learned these youngsters and their mothers had to walk up to twenty miles to fetch water. And then it was muddy. Sometimes it came from the same watering hole that their goats, cattle and camels used.

No wonder the children were dirty! Other tribes have disparaged the Turkanas because of the way they dress and smell. But if I lived in this arid land my water would be too precious to bathe in daily. That night I wept in shame for the arrogance of my tribe, the Kikuyu, and of others who have better land.

As we arrived at Lodwar late that evening I wondered what I could do about the water situation. The Lord knew I had no way to help, and that our new fellowship of churches had no money to spare. But I had no peace about it.

"Lord," I said, "I can never return to this hot and dry place unless You give me a way to supply water to the people. If You will give me enough funds to drill at least one bore hole, I'll come back."

Two and a half years ago, while visiting America on a preaching tour, I told an Ohio church about my burden for the Turkana people and their water situation. A few months later two men phoned me, asking to go with me to Turkana.

I was thrilled to think I could now return to that province with the hope of giving the people both physical and spiritual water [*interdependence*]. How interesting that our fellowship is called the "Fountain of Life."

When these two brothers traveled with me to Turkana they were like the Samaritans who became more excited than the woman at the well about the ministry of Jesus (John 4).

"When we get back to the USA," they told me, "we'll start fundraising for a water project!" [*symbiosis*]. As I write, the drilling rig is ready for shipping and we're just waiting for official approval from the Kenya government. Better still, we'll drill not just one well but many. Already we have enough encasements and pumps for four bore holes.

Meanwhile I talked to my friends about sponsoring small church buildings among the Turkana people.

"You've already helped us by paying off our church land and building in Lodwar," I said. "How about we build a church at Nadwart, the site of our first water hole?" [*multiplication*]

Again the Lord supplied the funds, and in April we will go with my friends from Ohio to dedicate the newly-built church at Nadwart. Isn't God great!

"I don't know what your destiny will be, but one thing I do know: the only ones among you who will be really happy are those who have sought and found how to serve." —Albert Schweitzer (1875-1965), German missionary and theologian.

For reflection/discussion: *What "drink of cool water" could your fellowship provide to a parched church in another country?*

STORY 3 — GHANA: NEW LEADERS ON BOARD!

It has been said that our leadership task is not over until we have trained our successor. An African pastor learned this from experience.

When our church started, a few leaders came from the mother church to assist us. Before long I noticed that these few leaders were monopolizing the leadership positions in the young church and that our own leadership base was not growing.

"Almost everything is being done by just a few people!" someone commented perceptively.

It got me thinking. How could we develop our own leaders to take over these roles?

After praying about it, I started a bi-weekly leadership class called "Spiritual Parenting" on Sunday mornings before the main service, and on Wednesday evenings [*energy transformation, fruitfulness*]. This was for the people who had just finished our new members' class and been baptized in water and joined the church.

Now most of the old leaders have left town because of work commitments, but as a result of the leadership training I did with the new members [*multiplication*], people are there to fill their shoes.

"The only preparation for tomorrow is the right use of today."

For reflection/discussion: In many churches most of the work is done by a small group of committed people. How can the leaders of a new fellowship ensure that the work of ministry is shared by all?

STORY 4 — GERMANY: CELL-BASED CHURCHES PRODUCE NEW LEADERS

Training new leaders is vital for the development of an organization, and these new leaders, in turn, need to train others to succeed them.

About a year ago our church held an important business meeting at which some major issues were brought into the open.

After a time of prayer the pastor put it bluntly:

"Our church has not been growing at the rate it should, for a congregation this size," he said. "In fact we've had no new members for more than fifteen months. I'd like to hear your honest views as to why this might be. As a leadership team we want to move forward, and we'd appreciate your suggestions."

Greta, who ran the children's ministry, spoke up first.

"You know what I think?" she said. "We should be evangelizing more, but we leaders are just too tired. Most of us need a break but it's just about impossible to get new people to replace us."

Wolfgang, who led the youth group, stood up next.

"I think," he said, "the church simply has too many programs consuming our time and energy. We're running so fast from one activity to the next that we're losing our sense of community."

"I agree," Martha said. "We're so stressed out that we don't have time to get to know our non-Christian neighbors — let alone invite them to join us."

"So what's the answer?" came a voice from the back. "Cancel all the programs? Just turn up every Sunday morning to sing? There's no community value in that."

"We'd have to continue the cell groups," Brigitte said. "If you're looking for community, they're at the heart of it."

The discussion continued over several weeks, with members being invited to think about the issues and present their ideas regarding the direction we might take.

After much prayer and debate we decided to move our church from being a program-based fellowship to being a cell-based one.

Through the NCD process we became aware that our minimum factor was in the area of loving relationships. But we've found that the structure of the cell church addresses two needs in this area: first, it encourages loving relationships in cells, and secondly, it apportions the leadership responsibility to more people. This leads to the spiritual growth of leaders and the overall number of leaders, as every leader has his or her apprentice [*multiplication*].

Transitions to new church structures are never easy, but if growth and better human relationships are a result, the risks are worth it.

For reflection/discussion: *What are likely to be the biggest challenges faced by a church that moves from a program-based model to a cell-based one?*

STORY 5 — ROMANIA: CATCHING A NEW VISION

"If people can't see what God is doing, they stumble all over themselves; but when they attend to what he reveals, they are most blessed." — Proverbs 29:18 (The Message)

When I was growing up my church had no vision for multiplication, nor did it have any provision for discipling (in small groups) or for training leaders. But when I, as a lay person, came to Timisoare I began to work in an evangelical student ministry where I was trained in evangelism, discipleship, leadership, small group leadership, and how to manage a para-church movement.

We student leaders used to meet from time to time to share our experiences.

"What I find frustrating," Alexei said one day, "is that we have all this training, all these new skills, and we can't actually put them to use in the church!"

Others agreed. They, too, had a vision that extended beyond the campus, but most of the leaders at the traditional old church (which had a membership of over 1000) were resistant to trying new ideas.

In the end my colleagues decided to start a new fellowship, so they would be free to work unhindered.

"Will you be part of our team?" they asked me.

I hesitated.

"I'll pray about it," I said.

And I did. But I felt no peace about leaving. In the end I chose to remain in the old church and to try to put in place a strategy of small discipleship groups along with a leadership training program.

My church has now, on its own initiative, taken strategic steps to encourage growth. [*fruitfulness*]. There were some changes in the leadership team, and the ministry of the church was structured into departments, with a team to be built for each of these.

The senior pastor began to share his vision from the pulpit, where he drew attention to the positive achievements of each department. He also made big changes in the worship services, with the result that the church now has a different atmosphere from formerly.

Our big need now is for leaders who can meet the needs of each department. So we are working to develop suitable training programs.

All these changes began three years ago. At that time we started to train the youth too, because the next generation of leaders is just as capable of ministering. We've sometimes met with opposition, but the church leaders realize multiplication is vital.

I am now working well with the pastors on the strategic planning team and I believe the "growth forces" will help us to minister better in the future.

"The vision must be followed by the venture. It is not enough to stare

up the steps — we must step up the stairs." — Vance Havner, American Baptist preacher

> ***For reflection/discussion:*** *What are the benefits of placing youth in leadership positions? What are the risks?*

STORY 6 — AUSTRALIA: WORKING SMARTER, NOT HARDER

> ***"Pass on what you heard from me... to reliable leaders who are competent to teach others." — 2 Timothy 2:2 (The Message)***

In conjunction with another parachurch ministry, we were asked to conduct evangelism training for the Rugby World Cup (RWC) to be held in Australia in late 2003.

During the early discussions someone suggested we offer a one-time training event which would equip people to share their faith during the RWC, but also for other occasions that might come up.

While most people supported this idea, others felt it was a little shortsighted.

Colin summed up the views of the latter group by referring us to 2 Timothy 2:2.

"How do we measure the fruit of any evangelism training?" he asked. "I don't think we should measure it by the number of people who can share their faith. Surely what counts is how many can train *others* to share it!" [*multiplication*].

So we decided to train up ten people who had a heart for evangelism. Each would be assigned a mentor who would work alongside them. This mentor would teach each student how to share their faith and how to pass on this skill to others. After being trained, each student would then be released into a church to train others, so that the processes could be replicated within different contexts.

The idea was that by the time of the RWC there would be multiple levels of training occurring across the city, as a result of the initial investment in the lives of ten people by ten teachers of evangelism.

Today, as never before our world needs disciples and disciplers. The harvest is ripe and the opportunities countless. But the method of fulfilling the Great Commission is through ***making disciples*** *who will in turn make other* ***reproducing*** *disciples.*

For reflection/discussion: *What are the qualities most needed in mentors?*

STORY 7 — NORWAY: OPTIMAL LEADERSHIP

On another continent, a pastor has realized there are at least two ways to function as a pastor. One of them is the traditional way, in which you do everything. The other is by multiplying yourself.

Multiplying one's leadership has to be better than doing everything yourself. If I think through my activities and priorities, I now realize it is the only way.

We've seen something of this principle of *multiplication* in our Alpha courses. In the winter and spring we ran a course in cooperation with some other churches. There were four groups and in one of them was a lady who believed in God but had never accepted Jesus Christ as her Savior. After making that commitment her life was transformed. After the course she attended a seminar to learn more about being a group leader. Now she leads a group and has a new assistant leader.

This way to multiply might not seem the fastest way to grow a church, but we've learned from long experience that it is the safest and best way.

I myself became a Christian when I was nineteen years old, and our pastor, who clearly understood the principle from 2 Timothy 2:2, gave us much time to grow. He not only taught us things but also showed us how to pass them on to others. Since practice is as important as theory, he took us out to evangelize in the town center.

Now in our church we ensure that the oldest children in the choir have the opportunity to lead it. That's leadership multiplication!

> *"The function of leadership is to produce more leaders, not more followers."— Ralph Nader, American consumer rights activist and lawyer, b. 1934*
>
> ***For reflection/discussion:*** *Why do some pastors find it hard to delegate some of their responsibilities?*

STORY 8 — RUSSIA: ALL PLAYING THE SAME TUNE

A church planter in Russia realizes he needs the members of the church as much as they need him. As he builds them up, so he is in turn encouraged by them.

I depend on my brothers and sisters in the church in times of need. From them I have learned how to pray and worship God. They include the special people in my life who have helped me to fight against sin and lay down the burdens I need not carry. They have also helped me to find a job and given me advice.

There's no way I could have started this church on my own. But others encouraged me, stood by me and evangelized. Still others translated for me, from a language that was unfamiliar. [*interdependence*].

Our music ministry is a good example of equipping leadership. I started out by playing the guitar myself. But when I entrusted the music and worship leading to others, younger Christians developed this ministry so it could become self-sustaining [*interdependence*]. At the same time they were able to grow in their own faith and draw closer to Christ.

We formed a small group which soon became so large that it had to divide. So we then trained one of the members to take over the leadership of the second group, which has a different age range [*multiplication*].

In small groups people can serve each other in various ways. For example, those who have the gift of music can serve by leading the worship. Members of a small group can also share their experiences and be inspired by the stories of others.

At a recent meeting our senior deacon asked a leading question.

"What really is our mission as a church?" he asked. "I think we need to agree on this and do some intentional planning."

How could we argue with that? The willingness is certainly there but we are not yet fully organized. We still need someone with the gift of administration to take care of scheduling, information and announcements. I suspect that person is just waiting to be discovered!

"Blessed are the poor in spirit." Admitting our needs to others is not easy, but it is essential. Happy are those who know when they are lacking and are open about it, for success comes to the ones who are able to ask for help

For reflection/discussion: *What three qualities do church planters need most?*

STORY 9 — GERMANY: SERVANT EVANGELISM

What do we do when a project we have high hopes for seems not to work out? Sometimes when there are few tangible results God is doing a work in us that will bear fruit in the future.

In May 2001 we planted a new church in Recklinghausen. From the start our focus was on evangelism, but because none of us had a strong gifting in that area, and because even the word tended to create feelings of anxiety in most of us, we discussed how we could do outreach in a way that was appropriate for us.

"Everything we do needs to be *fun*," Hilda insisted.

"The risk factors need to be minimal," someone else murmured.

"Whatever we do, it must serve the people of this city and bring a bit of joy to their lives," said a third.

"And don't forget," the administrator pointed out, "that everything we do must be achievable within the limitations of our time and abilities, given that we're a small team with limited resources."

We discovered in "servant evangelism" a tool that seemed to meet all those criteria and was appropriate for our city. Because two of our people wanted to get into evangelism right away, we could aim for *multiplication* from the start. Their task was to develop the concept, introduce and explain it to others, and be ready to field any questions. In this way a practical project could be planned and carried out.

After the concept was explained and understood, everybody agreed it was worth our efforts [*interdependence*.] We simply needed everyone's commitment to get involved.

Throughout the year that followed we went downtown to offer people coffee, cakes, toys, flowers, and so on. Sometimes we did small activities such as providing games for children, wrapping Christmas gifts for free, and praying with people.

It turned out to be such a positive experience for our team that even those who were against evangelism became motivated and began to join in regularly.

When the gifts of the people on our team (service, help, mercy, creativity) matched the needs of the citizens of our city (to talk, get help, experience friendship, see kind people, etc.) there was *symbiosis*. And so we began to develop a positive image with the townspeople.

"Oh, I know you," they would say. "You're the people who are often in our square, right?"

Things began to unravel, however, when new people joined our team who were not satisfied with giving out tokens of love to people but wanted to get them into our church "at any cost." Soon our group began to feel nervous, and people who had been relaxed in the beginning suddenly felt under pressure to produce quantifiable "results." So their enthusiasm and excitement began to wane.

We had neglected the principle of *interdependence* by assuming the new team members would automatically understand what our ministry was about. It was only after some painful conversations that we were able to clarify what the basic requirements and tasks were.

What has been the upshot? On the one hand the lack of conversion growth in our church has continued to motivate our team members to try new forms of evangelism; on the other hand we've learned much about the city in which we want to grow our congregation. We have also observed an increased trust and intimacy within our team (many didn't even know one another in the beginning) and through this a stronger sense of belonging ("*We* are planting a church together.")

Even our praying took on a new dimension — for example, we started to pray together while walking through the city once a week — and this encouraged us spiritually.

As for evangelism, to be honest we failed in our efforts to reach our part of the city. Ringing door bells and asking people if we could do something good for them or give them something just didn't work. In hindsight we were not able to transform our negative experiences (rejection, unopened doors, stupid remarks, lack of interest, fear of lost privacy, etc.) into something positive [*energy transformation*].

Also I overlooked the principle of *symbiosis* when I underestimated the need of our team to do something together rather than just walking door-to-door in pairs. Furthermore we lacked *interdependence* because we tried to implement our ideas of *multiplication* before all our people identified with it.

We did what we did because we believed that people whose needs were met and who were touched by divine love would sooner or later get involved in our fellowship and become interested in God. We did meet the needs of people (at least those in the streets) and we had good conversations with them, but there were no results as far as church growth was concerned. The challenge has been to persevere in faith that our efforts will bear fruit eventually.

There's been the temptation to use this ministry only as an opportunity to invite people to our Alpha courses, or as an excuse to cancel other things. But in the end our encounters with unbelieving people have motivated our teamwork, our belonging, and our spiritual growth. And who knows how God might work through us in the future?

> *"We each carried out our servant assignment. I planted the seed, Apollos watered the plants, but God made you grow. It is not the one who plants or the one who waters who is at the center of this process but God, who makes things grow. Planting and watering are menial servant jobs at minimum wages. What makes them*

worth doing is the God we are serving." 1 Corinthians 3:6-9 (The Message)

For reflection/discussion: *What important lessons might have been learned from this experience?*

STORY 10 — NORWAY: CHILDREN OF PROMISE

A disciple is one who undertakes the discipline of his/her teacher. Thus, discipleship is about learning how to follow... It's part education, part mentoring, part apprenticeship, but it goes a step beyond all of those. Disciples not only take in what they are taught and what they learn from being with the teacher, they take it into their core identity, so it defines who they are. — Robert Longman Jr.

In one area of our church life the principle of multiplication is functioning well. We could certainly do a lot more, but we've made a start.

We have a group of young people all aged about twenty years who lead our teenagers. They model caring, Bible reading and friendship as they spend time with these younger ones.

The teenagers themselves are helping in our Sunday School, or "Promise Land" as it is called. We teach them to befriend these children, to watch them, pray with them, visit them and spend time with them.

So we are seeing our young people discipling the teenagers, and then the teenagers discipling the children. That's an example of multiplication!

Christians have never changed the world – only disciples have. While the cost of discipleship is high, the rewards are great.

For reflection/discussion: *Who mentors the teenagers in your church?*

STORY 11 — AUSTRALIA: USING OUR GIFTS FOR BEST EFFECT

To know our gift and then to discover the sphere in which God wants us to use it is one of life's greatest joys. May it be our good fortune to help others to do both.

My four-year-old home church (which is also one of the churches I am coaching), had a minimum factor of Gift-Based Ministry. How could we overcome this?

"Let's run a 'Discover Your Ministry' course," suggested one of the elders. "I've heard that Saddleback Community Church in the USA has some good material."

"Oh, but that's an American program," someone else objected. "It probably wouldn't work in our context."

"Well, we could modify it for our situation," the elder continued. "I think it's worth trying."

So we agreed to give the course a try. In doing so we were able to harness the growth forces of *interdependence*, *multiplication* and *symbiosis*. My task was to model the running of this course and at the same time train someone to take over from me [*multiplication*].

The initial course was run at a leaders' retreat, and a key part of the teaching was to highlight the uniqueness of each individual in the body of Christ, and the powerful impact made by our differences when we worked together [*interdependence, symbiosis*].

The result? Some people were confirmed in their ministry, some decided to make changes, and many discovered aspects of themselves and their ministry which they had never considered before. The trainee leader went on to teach the course to a home group, and was planning to introduce it to other home groups in the church.

We are awaiting the next NCD survey to measure the impact of these growth forces, but we know they've made a significant difference.

Every Christian should understand the way he or she has been gifted and then put those gifts to use in ministry. Having been made for God's pleasure, we can then live to his glory.

For reflection/discussion: Are gift-based ministries operating in your church? If this is a weak area in your fellowship, how could it be developed?

STORY 12 — NORWAY: MAKING THE CHURCH MORE INTIMATE

"Everything in life revolves around relationships — everything. The most important relationship is a personal relationship with our heavenly Father through his Son Jesus Christ — a vertical relationship.... And the best horizontal relationships are covenant commitments to live with others, to become connected with others in a basic Christian community." — Rick Diefenderfer

When we did our first church profile four years ago, our minimum factor was holistic small groups.

This was a wake-up call to us Methodists, as historically our movement was built on small groups or "class meetings." So it was quite embarrassing to have scored so low (only 26) in this area. It was clear we needed to work on this principle as a priority.

Three and a half years ago we started a kind of pilot project. We had two goals: first, we wanted to develop a genuinely holistic small group; and secondly, we wanted to learn how to build up similar groups within the church.

Beginning with three men and myself, after six months we were ready to start our first proper group (with eight people) and to build up groups by the principle of *multiplication*.

The target of the first group was to multiply it into three new ones. So at the outset I picked two people to be the leaders of the groups that were to follow.

We then started on-the-job training of the new leaders, and after about six months we felt ready to launch the three new groups. Even before we finished the first group, the two leaders had started to invite new people to join their groups. Each leader also had to choose an apprentice from within their group.

We decided all the groups should have four core values — fellowship (with the Lord and with each other), ministry, growth and evangelization — but each group made its own decision regarding when and where and how often to meet.

After a year or so all three groups multiplied, and between twelve and eighteen months later the six new groups multiplied again. One group actually split into three. So now we have thirteen groups, and our score in 2002, on holistic small groups, was 75! [*multiplication*]

Clearly this principle of multiplication has worked well for us, although to be honest the youth groups present more of a challenge. So far I've not managed to implement the principle with them, but I'll keep trying. It may be a story for the future!

> *"Let's see how inventive we can be in encouraging love and helping out, not avoiding worshiping together as some do but spurring each other on, especially as we see the big Day approaching." — Hebrews 10:25 (The Message.)*
>
> ***For reflection/discussion:*** *Suggest some reasons why this pastor faces a greater challenge when working with small groups for youth.*

Growth Force Analysis of this story:

Out of his dismay over the church profile which revealed holistic small groups as a minimum factor, the pastor made the decision to build up his small church using the principle of multiplication. So he started with a group of eight people — and within three years at least thirteen groups had arisen from this process of multiplication.

What can you do when you don`t see growth happening at your church? You could say, "Well, it's better to add a few people from the outside, occasionally, than have no growth at all." But just adding new people to your team will not help your ministry to really grow. The way to understand growth is to see it as something that happens from the inside. You might not even notice it at first, but eventually it brings much fruit. If we believe in this kind of growth, we invest in multiplication. The pastor in our story was wise enough to give this strategy a solid footing — that is, he considered other growth forces during the whole process. He trained two other leaders (*sustainability*) and documented how the groups grew (*fruitfulness*).

"We felt ready to split," he writes, implying that they shared common goals. ("*Our* target was three groups.") We can infer that he was communicating interdependently with his team. This reduced the likelihood of rash decisions, break-ups or unrealistic goals. He also built in core values that helped the groups to exist interdependently.

One of the most interesting parts of this story is the end, and we can learn much from the writer's honest comment. He admitted he had tried the same approach with the youth groups — and it hadn't worked. Which shows us one more important truth: a genuine multiplication strategy is not necessarily replicated in a different ministry — because multiplication is not copying!

No growth force contradicts another. So if a ministry has been multiplied successfully and I want to start a similar process in another group, I need to remember that multiplication retains the value of variety, as we learn from the principle of symbiosis! Natural multiplication encourages interdependence as we seek to understand how a particular strategy could affect another ministry in the long term. It uses the energy of the multiplication process to spark another effort, but without appealing to people's guilt. ("You have to do things this way. Don`t you want to see your ministry being multiplied?")

In a healthy multiplication process we will ask people about their personal needs and ministry purposes (*fruitfulness*) rather than foisting a strategy on them just because "it worked" in another area or because we're keen to brag on statistics.

Multiplication simply means paying heed to a few questions, and resisting the temptation to "addition" for the sake of long term benefits. So a natural "multiplication all by itself" approach — balanced with other growth forces — has unique results. Here are some questions, which were all considered in this story:

- Will it increase production capacity?
- Has the possibility of multiplication been deliberately built in?
- Is the basis for this step the concern about a slow beginning?
- Is the motto "Addition rather than no growth at all"?

GROWTH FORCE 3:

ENERGY TRANSFORMATION

Energy transformation has two aspects: 1. Using the positive forces that God has already made available in a given situation (e.g., the spiritual gifts of believers), 2. transforming negative forces into opportunities for the Kingdom of God. But what sounds easy in theory can turn out to be difficult in reality. We need not only the ability to think creatively, but also the guidance of the Holy Spirit. This principle makes it clear: applying the growth forces is not a human undertaking but a Spirit-led process.

STORY 1 — SOUTH AFRICA: A CHURCH BREAKS OUT

"It seems to me that energy transformation is probably one of the least-known church growth principles of all, yet its consistent application could help churches in crisis more enduringly than many popular growth gimmicks." — Christian Schwarz, in ***Natural Church Development****.*

Our fellowship began as a house church in 1997. There were about thirty of us who had mostly come out of highly structured churches and were longing to experience more of God's Spirit. As a group we were committed to arranging camps where many people were liberated from bondage.

It was at one of these camps that we heard about the principles of natural church growth for the first time. Our NCD coach challenged us to have a survey done. The results predictably showed functional structures to be very low, but gift-based ministry was the lowest, at 14. The only score above 65 was in the area of loving relationships.

We decided to use our strongest characteristic to address our weakest; and it was at this point that we experienced the greatest opposition. When we started introducing the principles of the three colors and the discovery of gifts, a few families opposed this almost violently.

"It's all so unnecessary!" they insisted. "In fact we think it's even counter-productive to the fellowship."

This negative energy forced us to come to a decision [*energy transformation*]. As a wise old deacon put it at a meeting soon afterwards:

"We have two choices, friends — either we follow the path of least resistance and accommodate these families by just carrying on as before, or we push ahead with the process and risk losing them."

"And all the others they're talking to," muttered someone else.

"What do you feel we should do?" the chairman asked.

After some discussion we decided to press on, despite the risk.

The result was immediate: four families left the fellowship, a loss which represented about one third of our members at that stage.

Our strongest characteristic, loving relationships, was being severely tested!

On the other hand the crisis served to strengthen even further the strong relationships that already existed in the core group. As a result this negative energy was turned against itself as the leadership resolved to push through [*energy transformation*].

Today, after having several confirmations from God that we made the right decision, our fellowship has more than tripled in size [*multiplication*]. More importantly, 80 percent of the people have discovered their gifting and personal change compass, and we have started interviewing individuals to match their gifts with ministries and tasks. During this year we plan to extend the gift discovery process to the cells and to the whole church.

There is an excitement and expectancy among our people to start flowing in the gifting God has given them so they can fulfill their redemptive purpose on earth.

And the families who left? I'm happy to report that relationships with them are slowly being repaired as they observe growth and life in the fellowship.

This church has observed the principle of energy transformation at work, and they believe both their minimum and maximum quality characteristics have improved because of it.

For reflection/discussion: *At first sight, it looks like this story is an example of fighting against resistance — instead of transforming it. Where do you see this church using positive forces and / or transforming negative forces?*

STORY 2 — NORWAY: TELLING THE CHRISTMAS STORY

Someone has said that difficulties are opportunities to better things; they are stepping stones to greater experience. Sometimes, like this Norwegian church, we can be thankful for some temporary failure in a particular area, for when one door closes another opens.

Back in 1990, in preparation for the Christmas holy days, my church wanted to share the nativity story with children in the local kindergartens. We simply wanted to visit these young ones to explain to them what Christmas was really about.

The problem was, most of the kindergartens wouldn't let us in and many parents were opposed to their children hearing about the good news of Jesus' birth.

At a coffee meeting after the worship service one Sunday, we discussed how we might get the message out.

"I've an idea!" said Maria, one of our more creative members. "Why don't we put on a Christmas play and invite every kindergarten child to come to it?" [*energy transformation*].

She said she would be willing to write the script, and her friend, a woman with theatrical experience, volunteered to work with her on the production. I agreed to serve as secretary for the project.

In mid-November we wrote to each kindergarten in the town, encouraging them to come to our Christmas event. We explained it would be a like a parade, with everyone wearing a costume. The children might be dressed as angels, shepherds, wise men, Joseph or Mary, and we would play and learn in the church.

A few kindergartens agreed to come out of curiosity. Groups of about twenty children arrived, accompanied by two to four adults. I met them and we gathered in a small building near the church. Then, in front of them all, I put on a Roman robe.

"Good afternoon!" I said to the children. "I am the Emperor Augustus and I need to find out how many people live in my big country. So I've ordered everyone to travel to the city they came from and write their name in our big book."

I continued, "I'll start with you people, gathered here."

I then asked each child his or her name and wrote it in a big book. The children enjoyed that.

Then I invited everyone to come with me on a long journey, 2000 years back, when everyone in the Roman Empire had to be registered in the same way. We would travel to a small country called Israel and to a small city called Bethlehem. In that city something great was happening at the time — an event that would change the whole world.

I invited three of the children to dress up as wise men from the east, because they saw from the stars that something special was about to occur in Bethlehem.

The whole group of us then walked towards the church.

As Augustus I rapped on the door, which was opened by the angel Gabriel.

Gabriel told his story and some of the children put on angel garments.

We continued into the church and some of the children became shepherds, dressed in blankets with towels on their heads. Then two kids became Joseph and Mary.

We ended up at the altar, next to which was a manger containing the baby Jesus. Joseph and Mary stood nearby. At the altar I read the story of Jesus' birth, and the children and adults realized they had traveled through the gospel.

Two years ago the mother of a five-year-old phoned me.

"I thought you'd be interested to know," she said, "that my child told me the whole Christmas story, including the roles of everyone involved!"

Today close to 500 children attend our annual Christmas play [*energy transformation*] and from October onwards the kindergarten teachers start asking us when they can come to see it.

Many of the adults have seen the play every year since 1995, when we started. And the kindergartens are now open to us at all times, allowing us to do whatever we want.

> *"When you obey God, he will accomplish through you what he has purposed to do... If you do not obey you will miss out on some of the most exciting experiences of your life." — Henry Blackaby, Southern Baptist preacher, USA (1935-)*

> **For reflection/discussion:** *This church came into a ministry for children that was greater than any they had imagined. Can you think of an example where God has brought unexpected blessings to your church when you acted in obedience to him?*

STORY 3 — USA: A RE-ENERGIZED CONGREGATION

The River Heights Vineyard Church understands how momentum or energy already flowing, whether positive or negative, can be redirected to accomplish God's purposes. As a new NCD coach, Rick Yonker is seeing the powerful things that can happen when churches adopt NCD principles.

"As people embrace the process, the process changes the people, and the people change the church."

After the River Heights Vineyard Church had been through its first NCD cycle, Rick Yonker's senior pastor called him in for a chat.

"You've been an enthusiastic participant in this program from the word go," he told Rick. "I'd like to see you become an NCD coach."

Rick wasn't sure he needed another commitment, but he attended Phases One and Two of the training and went on to facilitate the church's second NCD cycle.

This time the minimum factor was gift-based ministry, with a score of 46, and Rick was by then the program's biggest promoter.

As he worked with the implementation team, Rick helped them to develop their strengths to improve their minimum factor. The church's highest scoring area was holistic small groups, and so the team decided to have every small group work through *The Three Colors of Ministry* by Christian Schwarz, a book designed to help people use their spiritual gifts to their full potential [*energy transformation*].

That experience led many group members to engage in a ministry that energized them and left them wanting to do more. The score for gift-based ministry went up 24 points — from 46 to 70.

Rick has since overseen the third cycle of the NCD process at the church, and scores have gone up markedly with each round.

A key to implementing NCD principles effectively is to commit to the process over the long haul. Once a church commits to doing NCD each year for three to five years, they can use it as a basis for strategic planning. When they work on their minimum factor for a year, the other seven key areas improve as well. But no quality characteristic functions in isolation. Individual units are connected to each other in a larger system, and changes in one ministry will affect other ministries in the church and community.

For reflection/discussion: *Why does using your spiritual gift energize you? Can you think of examples where this has happened in your life?*

STORY 4 — GHANA: FROM DEATH — NEW LIFE!

"Unless a grain of wheat is buried in the ground, dead to the world, it is never more than a grain of wheat. But if it is buried, it sprouts and reproduces itself many times over." — Jesus' words to his disciples. (John 12:24-The Message)

In the middle of last year one of the youth leaders in our district, Yosef, died suddenly. He came from a village twenty-two miles from ours and was an active and committed member. In fact he had wanted to plant a church in his village and plans for this were under way at the time of his death. What were we to do? Should we just allow his hopes to die with him?

"No!" said an elder emphatically. "Let's use the occasion of Yosef's death to further his vision." [*energy transformation*]

Yosef was to be buried in his village, and together with the other branch churches we organized a funeral for him. The sermon was strongly evangelistic, and now a good church has been planted in this village, with two leaders taking care of it. Far from letting the vision die, we used the occasion of this youth leader's death to plant a new church.

"Ultimately-it's not about us. It's not about me. It's not about my circumstances. It's not about whether I survive. Ultimately, it's all about Him. It's about the glory of God and His purposes being fulfilled in this world." — Nancy deMoss, teacher and author

For reflection/discussion: *Can you think of other examples, today and in the past, where God's purposes have been fulfilled through the death of his servants?*

STORY 5 — COSTA RICA: MAKING A JOYFUL NOISE

It has been said that creativity can solve almost any problem. Here a pastor turns a difficult situation into one which benefits both the church and the community.

Pastor Carlos' church had done a survey and we were working with him in the NCD process. One day he phoned me in some agitation.

"During last Sunday's morning service," he explained, "we had a visit from that neighbor I was telling you about. He disrupted the worship service, yelling that his patience was running out because he found the church's noise intolerable."

He said the man had even threatened to take the church to court in an effort to get the authorities to close them down.

"And he's violent," Pastor Carlos added. 'What are we going to do?"

I thought for a moment and then answered:

"Carlos, do you think that maybe we could take advantage of this situation, and that God might even be behind it?" [*energy transformation*]

The pastor didn't seem too convinced.

"Let's look at this from another point of view," I continued. "This man has already confronted you several times, but this time he did it before the whole church. At the same time, this man is partly justified. Your church building is still under construction. It doesn't have a ceiling, and that's where most of the sound is escaping to the neighbors on your boundaries."

"You're right," he admitted.

"Look, Carlos," I said, "why don't you take advantage of the situation, since now the entire congregation is aware of the problems you're having with this man? You could use this to motivate your members this Sunday. If they would give additional funds the building project could be finished and the ceiling completed so the noise would be eliminated."

"You're right!" Carlos grinned. "I'll do it!"

That Sunday Carlos invited the congregation to make a special effort and a short-term commitment to solve the problem. That very morning one church member gave $1,500 dollars, and the rest of the money came in over the next two months. In this way they were able to finish construction and solve the noise problem.

Pastor Carlos may not have realized it at the time, but I was applying the growth force of energy transformation to the situation. Instead of there being a court case, the energy of the angry neighbor was transformed and used to bring blessing to the church.

"When the solution is simple, God is answering" — Albert Einstein, German-born American physicist (1879-1955)

For reflection/discussion: *Is there a problem you are dealing with in your church that could be solved by the principle of energy transformation?*

STORY 6 — NORWAY: ACCOMMODATING DIFFERENT PERSPECTIVES

Because a church is the body of Christ, it functions best when all its members are able to share what they sense God wants the church to be and do. This Norwegian church found a creative way to solve the tensions that can arise when perspectives differ.

Our church serves a geographical area which includes several surrounding villages. As the congregation grew, more and more people wanted to use their gifts of teaching, encouragement, preaching, etc. So in order to release more people into ministry, more and more members were given the opportunity to practice these servant gifts during the worship services.

This did, however, create problems, as the services became longer and longer. For some of the parents of small children and those in charge of children's church, they were now lasting *too* long, and people were growing impatient.

In addition, our services were becoming increasingly ad hoc, which lessened their appeal to visitors. Over time the worship service became a bone of contention, since people had differing expectations as to its content. The families felt they were becoming hostage to everyone who wanted to exercise their gift in the worship service.

The elders decided at one of their meetings that the situation needed to be turned around — urgently.

"Couldn't we de-centralize?" someone suggested. "Why not run small groups in the various villages around here, so we can reach out to those in the immediate neighborhood?"

"That would mean an even greater time commitment!" another protested. "We already spend too long at church as it is."

"We hold our worship service *every second* Sunday," someone else suggested, "and then we could run more events locally." [*fruitfulness, energy transformation*]

Members agreed this might work, and so we decided to give it a year's trial.

It worked beautifully, because more people had the opportunity to practice their teaching, worship-leading and practical ministry gifts. The local gatherings soon became centers for training and equipping people, while the worship services became more gift-based. So the quality of the worship services improved and attendance increased.

Members were happy and eager to serve in the church, and it became easier to replace people who moved out of the area, since more people were now trained to take responsibility.

During that year we achieved a good balance between local small groups and the fortnightly celebration service in the church. New people joined the congregation (including many non-churched ones) and the duration of children's church corresponded more closely to that of the worship service.

> *"Because each believer is added by God to the body of Christ, he or she is interdependent on other believers to function correctly in that body. You cannot know God's will for your involvement in the body of Christ apart from the counsel God provides through other members." (Henry Blackaby, Southern Baptist preacher.)*
>
> **For reflection/discussion:** *Think about times and ways God has spoken to you through other believers, and thank God for using*

them to speak to you. What are the greatest hindrances to our hearing from God through other believers?

STORY 7 — NORWAY: HAPPY BIRTHDAY!

According to Mark Mittelberg, associate director of the Willow Creek Association in the USA, "One of the primary ways to please God is to raise the priority of finding lost men and women, who matter deeply to him, and to present his message to them in understandable terms, using relevant illustrations and effective modes of communication. All of this is with a view to removing unnecessary barriers and helping these people in their journey toward Christ."

The congregation in this story found a creative way to bring seekers into their church.

Our church members are enthusiastic about evangelism, as I am, and we'd been looking for ways to make it easier for people to come to church. How could we make church a non-threatening experience for people who rarely crossed its threshold?

At a church meeting where this was discussed, Gertrud, the director of women's ministries, came up with a new idea.

"Everybody has a birthday," she pointed out, "and everybody loves a birthday party. Couldn't we get some mileage out of this?"

This got us thinking. Gertrud was right about birthday parties being popular. Not only that, but they could be held in many settings other than people's homes — for example, in restaurants or rented halls.

So we set to work to make this universal human event a means of outreach. Now when someone in the church has a birthday we invite everyone in their oikos (sphere of influence) to a party. The invitation reads:

"My birthday is this week and I'm going to celebrate it next Sunday. I would be so pleased if you could come. At one o'clock we'll have a dinner followed by birthday cake. However, we usually have a service in our church earlier in the morning and I would be delighted if you would attend the service with me as well. Of course if you cannot get to that you are still very welcome just to come to dinner at one."

Then we put on a special "seeker service" for that day [*fruitfulness*].

We've found that about half of the people invited (many of whom have never set foot in a church before, except for weddings and funerals) come to the service. When the teenagers invite their friends the percentage is even higher. And it's great to see fourteen- to sixteen-year-olds sitting at the edge of their seats just soaking up the gospel [*energy transformation*].

> *"There is no doubt that creativity is the most important human resource of all. Without creativity, there would be no progress, and we would be forever repeating the same patterns." — Edward de Bono (b. 1933), historian and creative thinker*
>
> ***For reflection/discussion:*** *Jesus said, "People who are well do not need a doctor, but only those who are sick." (Matthew 9:12, TEV) Suggest other creative ways you could bring unchurched people to hear the gospel preached.*

STORY 8 — CZECH REPUBLIC: "NO RUSTY GATE"

> ***"If I speak with human eloquence and angelic ecstasy but don't love, I'm nothing but the creaking of a rusty gate," according to Eugene Petersen in his paraphrase of 1 Corinthians 13:1 (The Message.) This church in the Czech Republic has proved it.***

Our church is small, with just thirty-five members and an average age of about fifty-five. A few years ago we went through a crisis which resulted in a group of young and active members going their separate ways. But even that setback helped to develop relational qualities within the church community that remained.

The kindness and love now evident among our people has enhanced communication within both the leadership team and the congregation as a whole [*energy transformation*]. One of our leaders, in particular, has a love for God and people which has inspired a willingness to work together for the common good. The kindness he shows to other church members and his deep commitment to the Lord have had a huge impact on our worship services. Indeed, we feel the presence of the Holy Spirit there.

Not surprisingly, new people have been drawn to our fellowship, and some have made decisions to follow Jesus Christ.

The children's and youth communities are also growing. I asked one teenager what attracted his age group to the church.

He thought for a few moments.

"I guess it's because the adults treat us as equal partners and give us space to grow," he said. "We feel accepted here."

In such an atmosphere young people feel free to express their views and are also ready to listen and accept advice. [*interdependence*]

We've noticed, too, that the community functions better when there is an organized roster for things like cleaning and bringing elderly members to the church. Regular communication has helped the prayer and training groups. When you add to this a communal Bible study, grounded in love, you can see how relationships are being strengthened. Knowing one another's strengths and weaknesses all leads to better cooperation.

These days we are focusing on discovering our spiritual gifts, within small groups that are sincerely seeking to know God's will. All participants have benefited, and we are encouraging any new small groups to follow the same plan. We long for all members to be filled with the Spirit and inspired to practical service for others.

It has been said that the quality of our lives is the quality of our relationships. This church has seen that loving relationships within the congregation made all the difference to its growth and effectiveness.

For reflection/discussion: *The above church was small (less than fifty members). Is a similar atmosphere possible in a church of 200? How could it be achieved?*

STORY 9 — NORWAY: A NEW START

Energy which is negative can be transformed into something positive. We don't just fight against it — we find a way to transform it!

Our church's first survey revealed our minimum factor to be gift-based ministry. To address this deficit we asked our coach to bring some teaching on the spiritual gifts, and then to lead members of the church in a gifts test.

Almost all the members took the test, and the elders set up a schedule to see gift-based ministries established within our congregation.

To make a long story short, we set a goal for a certain percentage of members to be helped into an appropriate area of service by a particular date. We also set dates for the completion of personal interviews with all of these people.

Unfortunately we did not manage to complete the project according to the promised schedule, which led to problems within the church and disappointed people grumbling among themselves.

At first the elders made excuses, which only created more negative energy. Then, during an elders' meeting, Karl, an older man, remonstrated with us.

"We need to acknowledge," he said, "that we have let our members down rather badly. We've broken our promises. In my book that's not just procrastination or weakness. It's actually a sin!"

We felt chastened. Karl was right. And the only way forward was to acknowledge our shortcomings openly.

At the November church meeting Pastor Sven stood up before the congregation.

"We have an apology to make," he said. "We've let you down in terms of the interviews. We promised you they would be done by the end of September and they have not been. We are sorry and we ask you humbly to forgive us."

You should have been there! We felt love and forgiveness from the church members, many of whom encouraged and prayed for us. And soon many of them were asking for prayer and help for themselves. [*energy transformation*]

As all that negative energy evaporated we felt a new level of trust and love within the congregation — which improved other relationships as well.

"Use your gifts faithfully, and they shall be enlarged; practice what you know, and you shall attain to higher knowledge." — Matthew Arnold, English Victorian poet, 1822-1888

For reflection/discussion: *Someone has pointed out that we can't undo anything we've already done, but we can face up to it. We can tell the truth, seek forgiveness, and let God do the rest. Discuss examples from your own experience.*

STORY 10 — GERMANY: GRIEF TRANSFORMED

Hostile energies can bring greater growth in church ministry and interpersonal communication than positive energies, if they are transformed constructively.

As a leader I encounter three sources of hostile energy within the church: gossiping, criticism, and a lack of love. How should I respond to these? At first I invariably feel frustrated. Lacking resilience, I experience the hurt and pain which not even Christians are immune from. So I have to deal with this hostile and destructive energy.

Many years ago I found some helpful advice in a book on the psychology of grieving.

"First we have to live through our pain," it said, "but the energy we put into grieving can be redeemed and transformed into a new beginning."

Over the years the pain I've experienced through gossip has, in a way, been God's pain too.

But I've learned from it, and so the hostile energy has made me better rather than bitter. It has pushed me to a greater dependence on the Lord.

Hostile energy can wound us to the core, but it can also draw us to God in the end and increase our humility. That's been my story.

Occasionally, disappointing experiences within the church have resulted in despondency, and it's often taken a while for this negative energy to be completely transformed into healthy growth.

We cannot deny grief. It's part of life. So when hostile energies result in grief for me I share this with God and with a few trusted friends.

"Lord, what lesson do you want me to learn from this?" I ask my heavenly Father.

Usually I experience his advice and look for ways to turn this hostile energy around. If I harness its power I can then, over days and weeks, channel it into my ministry. It shows first in my character and later in my leadership.

> *"I have learned through bitter experience the one supreme lesson to conserve my anger, and as heat conserved is transmitted into energy, even so our anger controlled can be transmitted into a power that can move the world." — Mahatma Gandhi (1869-1948), Indian leader internationally respected for his doctrine of non-violent protest.*
>
> **For reflection/discussion:** *What negative experience in your life could you turn to profit and how?*

STORY 11 — AUSTRALIA: FEELING USEFUL

> ***"It is God himself who has made us what we are and given us new lives from Christ Jesus; and long ages ago he planned that we should spend these lives in helping others." — Ephesians 2:10 (TLB). That's why a sense of usefulness is essential to our well-being.***

Alan, a denominational executive, was keen to become a member of a local church. He made enquiries to the pastor of one church but was asked not to attend.

As a result the executive felt disenfranchised.

"It seems so unfair," he complained to a close friend. "I've had all this experience which could be used to help extend the Kingdom of God and yet it seems nobody wants me."

Alan then approached another church pastor, who accepted his membership somewhat reluctantly. But he was still not utilized in any significant way within his area of giftedness, and began to feel increasingly despondent.

He came to me, another pastor, and shared his frustrations.

"I sense I'm not being used," he said, "but I don't know what to do."

I saw an opportunity to harness Alan's significant negative energy and transfer it into a positive at the local church level. [*energy transformation*]

I invited him to share some of his experiences concerning empowering leadership at my church. His sense of value increased and he now says he wants to exercise his ministry gifts at the church. These days he is keen to continue investing his all for kingdom growth. His energy is being applied to building up, at the local level, rather than tearing down. (2 Cor. 10:8; 13:10).

> *"The purpose of life is not to be happy. It is to be useful, to be honorable, to be compassionate, to have it make some difference that you have lived and lived well." — Ralph Waldo Emerson, American poet, lecturer and essayist (1803-1882).*
>
> **For reflection/discussion:** *What God-given ability or personal experience can I offer to my church?*

STORY 12 — NORWAY: THE WORSHIP WARS

Face-to-face meetings are sometimes the only way to resolve difficulties and transform energies, as this leader discovered. When conflict is handled correctly, we grow closer to each other.

In 1999 our congregation had as its minimum factor Inspiring Worship. After some discussion we decided to bring together teams to prepare and lead the worship for a year. Each team included an elder, a deacon, a prayer leader, a leader for the children, and a teen-ager. As they planned the worship together they decided they wanted more services in the afternoon and more drama and new songs and music. The board of elders agreed, and we made some changes to the traditional services. [*fruitfulness*]

As time went on a group of elderly people began to miss the old services.

On their behalf Mrs T. wrote a letter to the board of elders.

"Dear Elders," she wrote. "Our group of seniors (aged sixty-five and up) are disappointed with the way the worship in our church has changed. While it may appeal to the younger generation, we are feeling increasingly left out and we are worried about the future of our congregation."

The secretary of the board read the letter aloud to his fellow elders.

"How should we respond to this?" he asked. "How can we honor these older people and somehow bring healing to the situation? I don't think a written reply will do it."

"I think we need to talk to these people face-to-face," said Jorg, "We need to take time to explain our policy and try to reach a common understanding."

And so we invited the senior group to a special dessert and coffee evening. They came and we talked. We discussed our vision for the congregation in regard to the Great Commission and our vision for the church's future. It was also an opportunity for us to pray with one another.

The meeting gave all of us a greater understanding, respect and love for each other. If we hadn't known about the growth force of *energy transformation*, the board of elders might have written a formal letter in response to the elderly members' concerns. But by talking things through we were able to leave one another in a spirit of good will.

We're still not in complete agreement, but at least we now have a common understanding of the church's goals and the will to see them accomplished.

"You can develop a healthy, robust community that lives right with God and enjoy its results only if you do the hard work of getting along with each other, treating each other with dignity and honor." (James 3:18 — The Message)

For reflection/discussion: *What am I doing to safeguard unity in my church fellowship today?*

STORY 13 — NORWAY: CUTTING THE APRON STRINGS

"Don't think only of your own good. Think of other Christians and what is best for them." (1 Corinthians 10:24 — NLT)

A group of people within one local congregation lived quite a long distance from the church. For many years they drove there regularly, but eventually they grew tired of all this traveling and sought a way to use their energy and gifts in the place where they lived.

The church decided to bless and encourage these people as they began to plant a new church in their neighborhood. It wasn't easy at the time, as the mother church lost a worship leader and a lay leader. But three years later the mother church is as healthy as ever, and the daughter church has grown bigger than the mother.

"Blessed is the leader who seeks the best for those he serves."

For reflection/discussion: *Is it time for my church to think about planting a new fellowship?*

STORY 14 — AUSTRALIA: I USED TO RUN THINGS

How often do we hear the old adage, "If you want something done right, you must do it yourself!" But this is poor advice — especially when it comes to church leadership, as Pastor Ralph Bowles discovered.

As the senior pastor of a church that has gone through significant conflict, I've struggled to develop a culture of excellence in the lay leadership. Negative experiences have created mistrust, and direct methods of control (for example insisting on reports) have only tended to make matters worse.

In the parish council we spent a lot of time in a workshop thinking about how to redesign our church management structure to make it more effective.

"Here's an idea," said one member. "Why don't we design our management around interdependent, overlapping teams? Each ministry team could relate with another team through a shared member. For example, the coordinator of the Sunday School program team could also be a member of the worship team that serves the family congregation." [*interdependence*]

The suggestion made good sense to us, and we decided to try it.

"The other issue I'm concerned about," I said, "is how to ensure the teams operate productively. A hierarchical structure doesn't seem to be wanted, but we do need some system of accountability."

"Written guidelines might be helpful," suggested Colin, the secretary.

And so he was delegated to draft guidelines for "Effective Ministry Teams."

We then asked each of the various interlocking teams to draft a simply-written Ministry Team Agreement.

Colin's ministry team guidelines made the team members themselves responsible for interdependence, evaluation, and fruitfulness, and they were empowered to do the work well. As leaders we did not design the evaluation procedures or other details but left them to the teams. [*fruitfulness*]

Because the whole process was thought up within each team, rather than being a directive from the top, it did not meet with the same resistance. [*energy transformation*]

I can see how powerful this process will be when it stimulates the teams to think and act interdependently with other teams and leaders. And as for me, as senior pastor, my load has been lifted. I've come to realize that my previous attempts to direct ministry operations failed because they simply didn't empower people.

The first Ministry Team Agreements are now being commissioned. I think of these guidelines biotically as the DNA for our church's teamwork, to be reproduced in the various "cells" of the church body.

Here is a pastor who realized his old way of doing things just wasn't working. The more he tried to lead from the top, the more resistance he encountered. Then it occurred to him that there was an alternative to the "top down" approach. By creating interconnected ministry teams and empowering them to devise and assess their own procedures, he found a renewed enthusiasm for ministry within his congregation.

For reflection/discussion: *Can you think of other situations in the church where better results are achieved by a team than individually? Are there any exceptions?*

STORY 15 — RUSSIA: CREATIVE PROBLEM SOLVING

*"Problems are to the mind what exercise is to the muscles, they toughen and make strong" said Norman Vincent Peale (1898-1993), an American minister who wrote **The Power of Positive Thinking**. Here we read of a church that turned a crisis into an opportunity.*

We were organizing the concert of a Christian band, Agape, which was going to perform in the biggest hall of the city. Most of the money had already been paid and advertising banners put up around the streets. But we discovered during the week before the concert that many of these banners had been pulled down. The problem was that an election campaign for the State Duma was going on at the same time and any kind of street advertisement was considered political propaganda, to be removed.

So the day before the concert we had no banners and no time to make any replacements. Plus we had a lot of money invested.

It seemed the devil had gotten the better of us.

Just before all this happened, however, we had been studying the growth forces and the brothers challenged me to apply these to the present situation. This was no easy task because we'd never been in this situation before.

Then Sergei, our marketing manager, came up with an idea.

"Why don't we just buy some advertising time on television?" he said.

It had never occurred to the rest of us, but anything was worth trying.

We put together a commercial that afternoon.

"Hey, Agape fans!" we said to the viewers. "The missing banners show just how popular this band is. Come to the concert, bring a banner along, and you'll get a prize!" [*energy transformation*].

The result far exceeded our expectations — the hall overflowed! So the negative aspects of the situation, with a little input from us, were used to transform the situation for maximum benefit.

> *Norman Vincent Peale also said that the "how" thinker gets problems solved effectively because he wastes no time with futile "ifs" but goes right to work on the creative "how."*
>
> ***For reflection/discussion:*** *In working out a solution to their problem, to what universal trait of human nature did these leaders appeal?*

Growth Force Analysis of this story:

What would you have done? After reading this story you might think the solution was easy. But it took courage to do what these people did.

A simple option would have been to give up. Advertising had already used up a lot of their money and other resources. So it would have been sad but understandable if those in charge had said, "That`s it — we've done our best."

But in our story the leaders did not answer a negative action with a negative reaction. Nor did they simply give up. Yes, they could have done something else. They might have bought new advertising, but the banners had disappeared the day before the concert, and so really there was no time, and possibly no money either. They could also have become consumed with guilt and questioned their whole advertising strategy in an unhelpful way.

Wondering how things could have been better is not the opposite of energy transformation — but many of us have felt discouraged when all we've received are questions and criticisms that have ignored our good intentions. The leaders in our story were still looking at their goal and purpose: by applying the principle of *energy transformation* they sought to discover how the loss of their banners could still help to promote the concert. They had nothing to lose, but their bold question was the beginning of an inspiring solution.

We can learn from this. We don't always need to come up with new energy. We may find another way to direct existing energy towards our purpose.

When your ministry faces obstacles, ask yourself: are there ways (persons, tools, media, communication) to channel this negative energy? Could it help or even inspire others to support your purpose?

GROWTH FORCE 4:

SUSTAINABILITY

2 Tim 2:2 is a great demonstration of this principle: "And the things you have heard me say in the presence of many witnesses entrust to reliable men who will also be qualified to teach others." It is important to Paul that Timothy invests in people who can invest in others. This is the principle of the next generation! Sustainability is about creating a never-ending ministry that starts with the end in view. It means checking every fruit for its seeds.

STORY 1 — NORWAY: PASSING ON THE TORCH

> *"You have a lot to give to many people — and a lot of joy to receive from imparting your years of experience-based wisdom. Show that wisdom by championing the rise of a few young leaders today. It's a win-win strategy." — George Barna,* ***Gracefully Passing the Baton***

The sustainability principle can be illustrated from the story of a farmer who prepares his son from childhood to take over the family farm. While still in his prime, the farmer hands over the property to his son when the time is right. Later the son begins to prepare the granddaughter to take over the farm, so the property can remain in the family.

Our congregation has used this principle with great success. For example in our scout program the future leaders are trained by the older ones so they can assume leadership when the time is right. Other groups in the church do this too.

> *"I start with the premise that the function of leadership is to produce more leaders, not more followers." — Ralph Nader (b. 1934), American consumer rights advocate*
>
> ***For reflection/discussion:*** *How do you ensure ongoing leadership in the various ministries of your church?*

STORY 2 — USA: CO-WORKERS IN CHRIST

> ***"I thank my God in all my remembrance of you, always in every prayer of mine for you all making my prayer with joy, thankful for your partnership in the gospel..." — Philippians 1:3-5***

Our church, Forest Hill United Methodist, has 850 members and an average Sunday attendance of 438. About a year ago we found ourselves floundering in our congregational life.

This came up for discussion at a staff meeting one Monday morning.

"We seem to be at a crossroads," I said. "We need a new focus in our ministry and mission. Anyone got some ideas?"

"I think Mt Carmel is going through a rough patch too," said Andy, our assistant pastor, who was known for his ability to think 'outside of the square.' "I'm wondering if we could somehow help each other?"

Everyone stared at Andy. Nobody had even considered working with the Mt Carmel United Methodist Church before. It was situated in a poor area and both attendance and morale were low. In fact the little church was in danger of closing its doors.

But the more we thought about the idea, the more interesting it became. Could we develop a partner relationship with this congregation?

Jenny, our office secretary, was always forthright.

"It wouldn't be easy," she pointed out. "We Forest Hill people tend to be Type-A, over-achieving, production-oriented people. It's a whole different ethos at Mt Carmel. So it might not work out. But there's no harm in exploring the idea."

"Before we contact Pastor Samuels, I'll have a word with the district superintendent," I said. "I'd like to hear what he thinks."

The conference office was very supportive, and before long we had set up a friendly meeting with Pastor Samuels to explore ways of working together.

The upshot was, we were soon able to link the resources of our two congregations, resulting in the renewal of both. Even Jenny had to admit her concerns were unfounded.

I find several growth forces at work in the life of our two congregations:

First, the principle of *interdependence*. As members and committees from the two congregations meet and interact, a larger entity is formed! This results in a positive ethos and witness to the congregations, as well as to the community at large as reports of this congregational partnership spread.

We also see the principle of *multiplication*. It has been well-stated that "the true fruit of a church is not a new group, but a new church." As Forest Hill has sent individuals and staff persons to Mt. Carmel, a new congregation is emerging and re-missioning. And we are finding a new vitality and purpose within Forest Hill.

Then there is the principle of *sustainability*. A good example of this is our sharing of Vacation Bible School resources. Forest Hill offered its Vacation Bible School curriculum, resources and some staff support so that Mt Carmel could hold its first Vacation Bible School in more than twenty-five years!

Of course the partnership has benefited both churches [*symbiosis*]. Mt Carmel has, for example, helped several Forest Hill members find a place to employ and deploy their leadership gifts. They have also reminded us, by example and identity, of the importance of a slower-paced, more personal approach to ministry than we were experiencing in the Forest Hill family. By rubbing shoulders and interacting with Mt Carmel, we have discovered a gentler, and more reflective style of ministry.

*Bill Hybels has written: "If only more leaders understood the distinction between 'just working with other people' and 'doing life deeply with one another as we serve together.' Practicing the latter approach could improve the relational temperature of every church leadership circle in the world." (**Courageous Leadership**, p. 74)*

***For reflection/discussion:** Is there an opportunity for your church to form a partnership with another local congregation?*

STORY 3 — NORWAY: RECRUITING NEW WORKERS

***"Take the teachings that you heard me proclaim in the presence of many witnesses, and entrust them to reliable people, who will be able to teach others also."** — 2 Timothy 2:2 (GNB)*

In our church we have many children and two different ministries to serve them. There is "Inka" for ten- to thirteen-year-old children (held on Wednesday evenings) and then there is the Sunday School. Each ministry has its own leaders.

Two of the four Inka leaders have been in this ministry for more than twenty years and have a real passion both for God and for children. In their ministry the "all by itself" principle has been evident for many years.

The adult leaders are always on the lookout for young persons in the church who need a task, and when they find them they invite them to be a part of the leadership group. In the beginning these young recruits come along just to watch and to have contact with the children and the other leaders. If they are interested they are then given more specific tasks. The leaders put a high priority on good relationships and on having fun together. So for many young people in our church, including myself, Inka has provided the first opportunity for leadership experience. Many have stayed in Inka for a year or so, and then moved into another ministry within our church or elsewhere. So leaders come and go, but the net result is that Inka is never short of leadership, because the principle of sustainability has been practiced for years. In fact new leaders are being trained up continually.

In our Sunday School we have the opposite situation. Although there are many leaders and many children, there are always too few workers. There is a tendency to look for new leaders only when they are needed, which is often too late. There seems to be no strategy for training new workers in advance of the need. So at the beginning of each new season there's a plea for new Sunday School workers, and often the panic-stricken Sunday School leadership team and church leaders have to come up with a short-term solution.

It must be admitted the situation is far from simple.

- Leading Inka is relatively easy, but Sunday School workers need the gift of teaching.
- Inka is on Wednesday evenings while Sunday School is held at a time when many people like to rest, spend time with their families, or do their weekend socializing.
- Inka's ministry is more about fellowship, while the Sunday School is more about Bible teaching.

That said, the principle of *sustainability* is still needed in our children's work — and for that matter, in all other areas of our church life!

"Success is where preparation and opportunity meet." — Bobby Unser, American racing driver, b. 1934

For reflection/discussion: *How does your church recruit its children's ministry workers? Do you struggle to find Sunday School teachers? What strategies have worked for you?*

STORY 4 — GERMANY: MENTORING YOUTH

"How lovely to think that no one need wait a moment. We can start now, start slowly changing the world. How lovely that everyone, great and small, can make their contribution...how we can always, always give something, even if it is only kindness" — Anne Frank (1929-45), German-Jewish teenager who died in a concentration camp.

Building up the church is hard work! Much energy must be invested to recruit and support co-workers for various ministries, and to equip them so they can in turn support others. As the oldest person in our congregation, I took this task upon myself. I first needed to ask myself, "What can I do in the time I have available? Where do I start? Which people shall I invest in?"

I lead a group in church which is responsible for praise and worship. I also have a passion for guiding young people during their adolescence and for that I need to spend time with them. The question was, how to put this all together.

My wife and I decided to run a Bible study for teenagers, along with their young leaders, Liwi, Alfred, and Jenny. We invited them to spend a Saturday evening with us, once a month. In our praise team there is another young couple — Robert and Katrin — whom we want to support as well. So once a month, on Saturday evening, we invite them all together to our home along with Liwi, Jenny, and Alfred.

We also invite Michael, who has a passion for evangelism, and hope that these meetings, and the support they offer, will produce abundant fruit [*sustainability*].

The greatest gift you can give someone is your time.

For reflection/discussion: *Where is it helpful to combine meetings and people, where is it counter-productive?*

STORY 5 — THAILAND: CHURCH PLANTING THAT WORKS

> *"Leadership should be born out of the understanding of the needs of those who would be affected by it." — Marian Anderson, American contralto, (1902-1993)*

I am pioneering a church planting movement in the northeastern rural part of Thailand. We want to see a self-supporting movement of local believers, multiplying churches throughout the area [*multiplication*].

To train the believers, I used to take them out evangelizing in the mission pick-up. But after four years I began to see a discouraging pattern emerging. If I didn't pick them up, they just didn't go out. Also, because the pick-up expense was separate from the church budget, we didn't think much about the cost. It looked as if we were going nowhere.

One evening when the church met to prepare its next budget, I offered a solution to our problem using growth forces.

"We need more money to finance our programs," the treasurer announced, "and we also want more control of the finances."

"I have a proposal," I said. "I suggest we take the transportation money used by the pick-up and give it to the church for you to budget. There will be just two conditions [*energy transformation*]. First, all church-related expenses, including my own evangelism transportation expenses, will have to come under the church's budget and jurisdiction. I'll limit myself to what you can duplicate-walking, public transportation or motorcycle [*multiplication*]. Secondly, the money will be released only through matching your local giving [*interdependence*] and that matching percentage will decrease by five percent a year over sixteen years."

They took a deep breath but accepted the proposal, which would bring them into a fully self-supported movement [*sustainability*].

We started with 20 percent of the budget coming from the locals and 80 percent from the mission. Now we're in our third year and church planting is being done fully by the locals, who are getting about by walking, motorcycles and public transportation [*fruitfulness*].

With excitement the believers announce each month their giving figures to be matched.

"The general giving has increased even more than our projected budget!" the treasurer commented with surprise.

To support new church-directed mission projects they are now mixing faith promises with their regular giving [*symbiosis*] and are even planning to multiply their movement into other areas.

Almost all of the growth forces are evident in this story. Progress occurs when a whole church, having caught a vision, is willing to share the responsibility for making it happen.

For reflection/discussion: *What was the most important lesson this missionary learned?*

STORY 6 — GERMANY: LIFE COACHES

A mentor is like a personal trainer who keeps you moving along your path and a sports coach who gives you feedback to help improve your game.

Years ago I attended a one-day seminar about building the church through mentoring. It seemed an interesting and important idea — something I wanted to apply without having to create specific mentoring relationships.

But like many a good idea, it remained just that. Nothing happened for years, and meanwhile the pleas of co-workers for mentors were becoming insistent. Still, other than having phone conversations, we did nothing about it.

I shared the matter during a staff meeting and everyone agreed on its importance, but the mentoring idea remained simply a vision.

As time went on we broadened our leadership structure to incorporate more staff. Every area of ministry would now have a consultant. But this was still not mentoring.

Then I attended some NCD training and experienced first hand the helpful guidance of a coach. During a meeting of home group leaders I finally offered help in the form of coaching, and shared my positive experience of this [*sustainability*].

"Would you be open to the experiment?" I asked them.

Not everyone was sure about it, but they were prepared to give it a try. We found a mentor for every leader, and the first meetings started soon afterwards.

It was a promising beginning.

At the next pastoral care meeting some home group leaders were present and I took the plunge again.

"I wonder if we could apply mentoring relationships to ministry teams?" I asked them [*sustainability*]. "If we could do this, existing relationships would be strengthened, and some of the assignments given by the coaches could be more focused."

Again, meetings began to happen.

"I have a lot of material on children's ministry," said one co-worker. "I wouldn't mind taking the responsibility for training and coaching in that area."

We worked out a plan from the materials available that could be applied to this specialized area.

In a relatively short time we've accomplished much more than we ever did during the years we were thinking about it!

> *"Do not wait for leaders; do it alone, person to person." —Mother Teresa (1910-1997), founder of the Missionaries of Charity*
>
> ***For reflection/discussion:*** *What step can I take today to connect with another believer at a more heart-to-heart level? (Rick Warren,* ***The Purpose Driven Life****)*

STORY 7 — GERMANY: AN ENDLESS LOOP?

"The best ideas are common property." (Seneca, 5 B.C. — 65 A.D. Epistles)

The best way to get an example of *sustainability* is to run a seminar in your church on the growth forces in general. You can then ask participants to give you successful examples of the principles at work, through letters or articles for the church newsletter.

In this way people can more easily understand the principles and you may even have enough material to publish a book on the subject from which others might benefit! [*sustainability*].

From the money you make, you or others can then run new seminars in churches where you again collect successful examples of growth forces in the form of articles... which you can then ...

Oh, you know what I mean!

(Actually we have thought of this... — Ed.)

STORY 8 — USA: KINGDOM PRIORITIES

Fundraising can bring unexpected benefits to a congregation, as this church discovered. Through an associated prayer emphasis it even led to spiritual renewal.

Our church is raising funds for a building. Many outside ministries exist to help with this, but most of them temporarily impose a new layer of organization during the project. We had to make a choice: would we raise funds by ourselves and risk a lower income, or would we seek outside help and risk losing our focus on reaching people? We chose the former because it allowed us to act biotically.

First, we used existing ministries to educate our people about the need [*sustainability*]. Secondly, we involved our small groups in a prayer emphasis which caused significant spiritual renewal [*energy transformation*].

Thirdly, by emphasizing kingdom growth above monetary growth, we have continued to do need-meeting evangelism. The result is symbiotic. Our numerical growth provides new resources to build, and firming up the building plans increases the enthusiasm of our church family to reach more of their friends.

Giving requires faith. When we share our resources, we show our trust in God's provision. At the same time our faith and reliance on God is increased when we are able to give and see God's faithfulness.

For reflection/discussion: *What factors most hinder a church from achieving its financial objectives?*

STORY 9 — GERMANY: PARTY TIME

"They committed themselves to the teaching of the apostles, the life together, the common meal, and the prayers." (Acts 2:42, The Message)

Our church has always been good at throwing parties. Our board plans at least four per year, but even if there were more we wouldn't tire of them. Celebrations are the best way to bring people together, and we'd like to use them to liven up even more areas of our church's ministry [*sustainability; symbiosis; energy transformation*]. We had a big party to celebrate the end of last year and our typist made a permanent record of the occasion. Otherwise much of it would have been forgotten.

The beginning of the church year is another cause for celebration. Guests show up, and we have to bring in more chairs. Last time we didn't have enough tables, and the trestles were groaning under all the delicious food people brought. Everybody made their best recipes and we had a variety of Russian, Polish, Greek, Dutch, Croatian, Saxon and other cuisine. Of course there were plenty of opportunities for creativity and humor, and delightful music was provided by flute, violin, guitar and mouth-organ. Even the clean-up, including the putting away of chairs, was a happy time. We enjoyed finishing off the tasty leftovers and playing hide-and-seek with the kids. People hardly noticed the lack of a dishwasher because there were so many helping hands. So the end was as satisfying as the beginning.

> *"Stop worrying about the potholes in the road and celebrate the journey!" — Barbara Hoffman*
>
> ***For reflection/discussion:*** *Is there a culture of celebration in your church? If not, what could you do to encourage one?*

STORY 10 — GERMANY: GROWING LEADERS THROUGH ALPHA

> *"Every form of organic growth sooner or later reaches its natural limits. A tree does not keep getting bigger; it brings forth new trees, which in turn produce more trees. This is the growth force of 'multiplication' which characterizes all of God's creation." — Christian Schwarz, in* ***Natural Church Development****.*

An example of *multiplication and sustainability* is seen in our work with Alpha courses. Almost without exception, leaders and co-workers in the current Alpha team have been participants in Alpha courses themselves. Over time they moved from being unbelievers to believers and then from believers to co-workers for the following Alpha courses. All of this happened when at the end of a course participants were invited to become involved as assistant leaders.

At the same time, our previous Alpha leader found a new area of ministry in which he began to serve and in which he has encouraged his followers to do likewise.

"Leadership cannot really be taught; it can only be learned." — Harold S. Geneen, English-born American communications executive, 1910-1997

For reflection/discussion: *Where do you see multiplication in this story? Where does multiplication turn into sustainability?*

STORY 11 — NORWAY: CONFIRMATION CLASSES

"There is no 'waste' in nature: Leaves that fall from a tree turn into humus and provide nutrients to support the further growth of the tree from which they fell." Christian Schwarz, on the principle of Sustainability.

Each year about a hundred young people come to our church to attend confirmation classes. The course lasts eight months, but traditionally very few of those confirmed have ever returned to the church afterwards.

Two years ago Maria, a young woman, took on the responsibility of training the young confirmation candidates. At the end of that year Maria invited her students to attend a training course the following fall to become co-leaders for the next confirmation classes [*fruitfulness*]. Out of one hundred people, fifteen said yes. Last year twenty-five young students attended the confirmation class, of which the earlier fifteen had become co-leaders. This has worked so well that we intend from now on to let earlier confirmation students become teachers for the new confirmands [*sustainability*]. They speak the same language and are in many ways on the same wave length as the young candidates.

"Train children in the way they should go, and when they are old they will not turn from it." — Proverbs 22:6. (NRSV)

For reflection/discussion: *How well does your church retain its young people, and what are some ways you might do this better?*

Growth Force Analysis for this story:

This story sounds so simple. With a great approach and an exciting end we would love to know more about what they did. We know little about Maria, the woman who started the training course. But a key to her success is found in the words "to become co-leaders for the next confirmation classes."

The all-by-itself principles can be indicators of faith, because if I want to apply them I am forced to look ahead and ask myself what I want in the long run. A healthy faith is developed, because the Bible instructs me to invest. True faith invests, gives away, gives to others and equips them. It doesn`t sit around waiting for a miracle. Jesus wants us to step out in faith and to invest — like him — in other people.

The principle of sustainability (formerly called "multi-usage") was often explained by the saying "killing two birds with one stone." But "doing more things at the same time" doesn't fully explain it. Sustainability involves a deeper purpose. When we deal with people, it is not so much about "killing two birds with one stone" as about avoiding "one-way measures" or "one-way energy investments." In fact it's about the maintenance and growth of our ministry!

Maria invested her time in developing co-leaders. She could have said, "What a waste of energy. It'll take so much of my time, and who knows whether they will ever be willing to share what they have learned?" But her experience proved that it was worthwhile to train those young people because their way of teaching would have a unique impact on the next generation of confirmands whose world they understood.

So the principle of sustainability encourages us to share our time in ministry with others who can learn from us for a specific purpose. We can bring out the gifts and potential of these other workers, and bring continuity to our ministry. As we train others for our role we also have a great opportunity to show authenticity as they get to know us and we get to know them.

Training is not an option for a leader. It is essential if we are serious about our ministry and its sustainability. Nor is saving energy an option. We must not waste our valuable time on any other activity when it could be invested in on-the-job training, as Maria in our story realized.

Do you understand the principle of sustainability as merely "killing two birds with one stone"? Or do you see the wisdom of this principle when you observe the positive impact of your actions on the original situation? Start to talk to your co-workers about the possibility of applying the sustainability principle with them.

Sustainability can also be the basis for *multiplication*. Once the young leaders have been trained and supervised for a certain time, they may be able to lead their own groups.

GROWTH FORCE 5:
SYMBIOSIS

Like interdependence, the principle of symbiosis refers to the church as the Body of Christ that has many different parts. While interdependence focuses on the question "How are the different parts connected?" symbiosis focuses on the question "How do the different parts complement each other?"

God gave us diversity. Believers are different, and people who are not-yet-believers are also different — in their personalities, in their working styles, in their hobbies etc. This has many consequences for Christian ministries. We have to overcome competition as well as the tendency to make everything uniform. And we have to use our diversity in symbiotic ways.

STORY 1 — NORWAY: COMPLEMENTARY GIFTS

In high school biology we learned about symbiosis — the situation where two (or more) plants or animals live together and need each other to survive. In a well functioning church we are likely to find examples of this same principle.

We know that for a church to thrive and grow, all the people involved must have a clear knowledge of what their gifts are, and their positions and jobs in the church must be based on these gifts. But I have come to realize that our gifts are not efficient unless they work in symbiosis with the gifts of other people [*symbiosis, interdependence*].

My gift set consists of leadership, teaching and prophecy. That means I understand just what needs to be done and how it needs to be done, but I am not that good at actually *doing* it. When I began to understand this, I looked through the list of people who had done the gift-test for themselves and found one person who had the gift of administration, with whom I knew I could work. This was Ingrid, aged 42, a longstanding member of our church.

Ingrid had worked for many years as an executive secretary in a local law firm, but she became expendable when the senior partner retired. Despite an impressive CV, for the past three years she had not been able to find a job that suited her qualifications and experience. Because she needed an income to survive, however, she was now employed as a sales assistant in the local clothing store — a job that gave her little satisfaction.

I invited her to come and see me one Monday, and explained my situation.

"Ingrid," I said, "I really need help. I need somebody with the gift of administration to get all the warrants we need for our outreach plans, to make contact with the right people in the municipal government, and basically to do a lot of the paperwork — because that's what my initiatives create! And I hate papers... I believe you are just the sort of person who could do this. Would you be interested?"

To my surprise, tears welled up in Ingrid's eyes.

"Pastor Nils," she said, "This is the job I've been waiting for — for years!"

Within weeks of her joining the staff it became obvious to us both that we needed each other's gifts to be efficient and successful in our ministries. Together we could achieve much more than had been achieved earlier [*symbiosis*].

"If I could solve all the problems myself, I would." — Thomas Alva Edison (1847-1931), American inventor, when asked why he had a team of twenty-one assistants.

For reflection/discussion: *Is there any job you are now doing that could better be handled by someone else?*

STORY 2 — GERMANY: "ROUTINE CHRISTIANS" NO MORE

"And the special gift of ministry you received when I laid hands on you and prayed—keep that ablaze! God doesn't want us to be shy with his gifts, but bold and loving and sensible." — Paul to Timothy (2 Tim. 1:6 — The Message)

One Sunday morning, a few minutes before ten o'clock, several parishioners were sitting in the pews of a small German church, waiting for the sermon. But even for those who were regular churchgoers and active in the fellowship, the fire of a passionate faith had long gone out.

The pastor had a name for those Catholics who lived the Christian life only out of duty. "Routine Christians," he called them.

However, within his two parishes, St Michael and St Pirmin (with a combined total of 2,500 members) the "routine Christians" would soon be in the minority.

After the pastor discovered Natural Church Development, he began a pilot project that he hoped would — in his words — combat the "inner emptiness and loss of Christian passion."

At the end of 2000 he initiated within his diocese a project which focused initially on twenty-four members of church boards and parishes.

"It's important for the leaders to get spiritually charged first," he said as he unveiled the plan. "This first stage of the project should take a good two years and then we'll see how things develop."

However, by the middle of the project exciting things were already happening in his church: people were communicating more openly, prayer groups were being formed, interpersonal relationships were being strengthened, and members were treating one another with greater understanding and respect [*fruitfulness*]. In short, they were coming alive.

"Before there was little difference between the church fellowship and a sports club," said one member. "But there's more to our faith now than just organizing parish festivals."

So how did this transformation happen to the people of his church?

Natural Church Development is about maximizing the existing potential of a church. An initial analysis showed that at St Pirmin and St Michael the minimum factor was passionate spirituality.

With the help of an NCD coach we developed a strategy to release into both parish churches a passionate spirituality and a faith life full of commitment and excitement. As a result four working groups were formed that approached spirituality from different angles [*symbiosis*]. At the core was a questionnaire through which all participants could discover and analyze their spiritual gifts and abilities.

We discovered that many who were gifted with skills or administrative abilities were not in their right place of ministry. Many were not even aware they *had* spiritual gifts. As a result of this initiative a process was established through which everybody could find their right place for ministry within the church body.

Another group focused on "faith goals." Had people been growing in their faith since confirmation? Everybody had some kind of Christian belief, but we discovered a lot of theological gaps. So the church organized Alpha courses to provide teaching in the basics, and the demand for these was high. We also ran a second course for other members of the congregation.

In addition many home groups were formed in which people sang together, prayed and shared their faith [*interdependence*]. Some of them had been backsliders.

"I was searching for a deeper kind of faith and it's exciting to be able to share this with others," one said.

Corporate prayer is no longer foreign.

"In our group it's become our habit to pray at the beginning," one young mother said.

At the same time she discovered there were few active churchgoers within the group.

To create a safe environment for other members of the fellowship a box was created where people could place their prayer requests anonymously [*interdependence*]. Once a month designated people from both parishes met and prayed for those people and their requests. More than a hundred requests, some very personal, were collected.

"It shows how much people long for prayer and personal intercession," the pastor observed.

Following all these positive experiences it was clear the natural development of the church needed to continue.

"We still have much to do," emphasized the preacher, "but I'm enjoying the work. In fact it's a privilege to be a minister in a community like this where the results are already measurable."

The second profile showed an increased score in passionate spirituality. The next areas they want to work on at St Ingberts are relationships and evangelism.

For reflection/discussion: What was the key to igniting passionate spirituality at this church?

STORY 3 — GERMANY: A WORSHIP TASKFORCE

"Help needy Christians; be inventive in hospitality." — Romans 12:13 (The Message)

"How can we make our worship more up-to-date and relevant?" the pastor asked his leadership team at the Tuesday staff meeting. We're starting to lose some of our younger people because they feel we're in a bit of a rut. They've even told me so."

"I don't think it's just the music," said Sophia, the evangelism pastor. "There needs to be more opportunities for fellowship afterwards. Some people go home after the morning service without necessarily being spoken to by another soul."

"Well, we can't just change the worship format overnight," said Christoph, the assistant pastor. "The older people appreciate the traditional hymns and they'd be up in arms. You wouldn't last long, Helmut."

"And these shouldn't be board decisions either," said Gerhardt, the board chairman. "I think it would cause too much resentment. People like to feel they've been consulted."

"Actually I don't think any controversial changes should be instigated from the top," Pastor Helmut commented. "They need to be owned by the entire congregation. And they need to be introduced gradually."

"Put it on the agenda for the next board meeting," Christoph suggested. "It might be wise to appoint a committee to look into this issue and find out just what people *do* want. And such a group could represent all sections of the church. "

The following month the church board appointed a special taskforce to handle the format and development of our worship [*symbiosis*]. On this team were two members of the board, the Sunday School superintendent, a member of the youth group and the leader of our hospitality ministry, and they agreed to meet twice a month.

The taskforce has been in place for six months now, and is working well. After discussion, the team brings to the board new suggestions regarding worship. The board then presents these new ideas to the congregation. In this way the church board is released from being responsible for the worship format, and the taskforce is supported in implementing its goals.

Following a suggestion from the taskforce a coffee ministry was set up. Now after each service people can stay for coffee, tea and biscuits and spend time with one another.

We've noticed attendance has increased and the worship itself is improving in quality because people are excited and motivated.

An old proverb says, "Who practices hospitality entertains God himself."

For reflection/discussion: *Does your church have a hospitality ministry to complement your worship? If so, how could it be strengthened?*

STORY 4 — AUSTRALIA: RESTRUCTURING FOR GROWTH

"Under Christ's control all the different parts of the body fit together, and the whole body is held together by every joint with which it is provided. So when each separate part works as it should, the whole body grows and builds itself up through love." — Ephesians 4:14 (GNB)

When we did our third profile, Functional Structures turned out to be our minimum factor.

Pastor Andrew Clark and his associate, Clive Wilson, were having a confidential chat in the senior pastor's study one Tuesday morning shortly after the results came out.

"Hmmm...." said Pastor Clark as he stirred his tea, "Looks like we've got some work to do in regard to 'functional structures' over the next twelve months. So where do we start, Clive?"

The younger man leaned forward.

"I think one of the problems is with the board of elders," he said quietly. "They're good people, and all keen on outreach, but evangelism is just one of the quality characteristics we're supposed to be aiming for. The home groups seem to be working well, but that's only by the grace of God. Perhaps we need some new people on the board — people with different passions."

"I think you may be right, Clive," said the senior pastor. "I think this is a matter we should put before the church at the next members' meeting."

The upshot was, the church did agree to restructure the eldership team so it better reflected the eight quality characteristics.

As each elder focuses on a different church health principle which he or she is passionate about [*symbiosis*] we now have a renewed focus on the "things that really matter" within our community of believers. If any one of these elements is lacking, our church is less than God wants it to be. And so as each coach works with the other coaches, all the essential elements associated with church health are addressed.

As one coach establishes a process or releases someone into ministry, other coaches are brought in to support this new initiative, but they also enjoy its benefits. No coach working in isolation could achieve the synergistic results that come from working together.

> *"Teamwork is the ability to work together toward a common vision, the ability to direct individual accomplishments toward organizational objectives. It is the fuel that allows common people to attain uncommon results." — Andrew Carnegie*
>
> ***For reflection/discussion:*** *Does the leadership structure in your church promote the eight quality characteristics? If not, how could it be modified for greater effectiveness?*

STORY 5 — ROMANIA: COMPLEMENTARY GIFTS

> ***"God put every different part in the body just as he wanted it to be. There would not be a body if it were all only one part! As it is, there are many parts but one body." — 1 Corinthians 12:18-19 (GNB)***

I arrived at the church in 1996, at the time of its dedication, when there were 65 members. Others before me had constructed the building. Now they needed a spiritual leader. My first sermon was about the transfer from Nehemiah, the builder, to Ezra, the teacher.

One day Boris, the chairman of the elder board, drew me aside.

"Would you consider a call to the pulpit?" he asked me quietly.

It felt like an honor to be asked, but I didn't need a long time to think about my answer. I was aware of my gifts and knew they did not include pastoral leadership.

"No," I said. "I don't feel this role is for me. My calling is more to be a visionary — someone who comes up with ideas for others to implement."

So the position was advertised and we prayed that God would bring us the right person for the job.

A few months later along came Vasily who had pastored another small church for seventeen years. Our church elected him as pastor and I was happy to join the leadership team as his associate.

There was a huge contrast between our personal styles. Vasily was quiet, calm and rather slow in making decisions, but he was very stable in the areas he knew well. I was the opposite: visionary, energetic and easily bored with repetitive tasks.

Together, however, we formed a great team. The church grew in seven years from 65 to about 300, six other churches were planted, and the youth ministry is now an important part of our work.

Boris, Vasily and I were having coffee recently, when Boris brought up the subject of our modus operandi as a leadership team.

"You know," he said, "in personalities you two guys couldn't be more different! But it's been wonderful to see how your diverse gifts have complemented each other." [*symbiosis*].

> *"No one can whistle a symphony. It takes an orchestra to play it."*
> *H.E. Luccock*
>
> ***For reflection/discussion:*** *Can you think of examples from your own experience where two dissimilar people have complemented each other in ministry?*

STORY 6 — USA: THE NETWORK COURSE

> ***God has given us talents for specific reasons. We need to use them for him and his glory.***

I had been hired as Bridgeway's part-time Ministry Coordinator for less than a year. For most of this time I had been studying, researching, and learning more about my role. As the Equipping leader for our church I was expected to prepare ministry descriptions, train ministry leaders, and recognize and encourage both leaders and ministry helpers. I particularly needed to promote the use of our God-given spiritual gifts in service.

Suddenly I felt overwhelmed by the huge responsibility laid on me. Not only were my paid twelve hours per week insufficient for the task, but I was well aware I didn't possess even half of the gifts or skills needed to work on all these areas. I was going to need much help.

I decided to start with a weekend seminar called Network, which would help others in the congregation to discover their spiritual gifts so they could be directed into appropriate areas of service (gift-based ministry). So I began to build a team to help me plan and implement this seminar [*interdependence*].

At the first meeting I invited several people to come and hear the vision of Network and the areas of ministry opportunity that were available. To my great surprise, everyone who came decided to join the team in roles that seemed to fit them.

That was when my true lesson in leadership started. I had read in my studies that true leaders equip others to use their gifts and to lead. These team members weren't there to "help" me; rather I was to empower them for service and leadership. In serving with these team members over the next four months, wonderful and exciting evidences of God's sovereignty began to unfold.

Three of the Network team members happened to be involved in ministries that coincided with the roles they had chosen on the team. Needless to say, when these team members were empowered they drew resources and skills from existing ministries to help make the Network seminar a success.

Joan, who had offered to be in charge of hospitality, bubbled with creative ideas.

"I'll get the hospitality team involved," she said. "We could create a good welcoming environment for the seminar, with a light meal and some bright centerpieces for the tables."

Diane, who had volunteered to head the promotion, was keen to recruit her theatrical ministry buddies for the task.

"We could put together a short drama for the worship service, a week before the Network course begins," she said. "We could tie it in with the course and with spiritual gifts."

Belinda, who was helping Diane with the promotion, said she would enlist the aid of her aesthetics team to create a beautiful visual prop. This would include every spiritual gift, and would catch the eye of everyone in the sanctuary.

Even more exciting to see were the Network participants who discovered their passions and spiritual gifts and were encouraged to use these in the various ministries of Bridgeway, including the hospitality, drama, and aesthetics ministries. [*symbiosis*]

> *"So since we find ourselves fashioned into all these excellently formed and marvelous functioning parts in Christ's body, let's just go ahead and be what we were made to be, without enviously or pridefully comparing ourselves with each other, or trying to be something we aren't." — Romans 12:4-5 (The Message)*
>
> ***For reflection/discussion:*** *Does your church empower its members to exercise their spiritual gifts in ministry?*

STORY 7 — GERMANY: RELATIONSHIPS ARE BETTER THAN PROGRAMS

> ***"I want you to know, my brothers, that the things that have happened to me have really helped the progress of the gospel." Philippians 1:12 (GNB)***

You might wonder how in a stuffy church environment two groups of Alcoholics Anonymous would get on. But both groups are growing strongly. When we started this ministry a few years ago there was one thing we were clear about: it was our ministry for others — something we were doing for the community.

Over the years we've been surprised when occasionally somebody from the AA groups has come to worship with us. And we've been amazed by their attitudes — the open, simple, sincere way they treat one another within the groups. In fact we've been keen to see the same thing happening within the church!

At AA everybody is accepted. They take care of each other, help each other, and are concerned for each other. Their language is plain and clear. They are ready to learn. They take off their masks. Such openness is what we need too.

We once thought it was we who were giving. We provided the spiritual nourishment after all; we wanted to show the purpose of life and to mediate hope. And we rejoiced that these spiritual impulses were being understood and accepted (for example, prayer and waiting for God's help.) But through our AA programs we have also discovered insights for our own spiritual development. We have discovered that relationships are much more important than programs. That's why we're inviting the members of both groups to the party we're holding in six weeks' time. It is great we can learn from them! [*symbiosis, interdependence*]

> *"Accept the place the divine providence has found for you, the society of your contemporaries, the connection of events." — Ralph Waldo Emerson (1803-82), American poet and essayist*
>
> ***For reflection/discussion:*** *If relationships are more important than programs, what could we do to promote more transparent relationships within our congregation?*

STORY 8 — USA: EMPOWERING LEADERSHIP

> ***"If you preach, just preach God's message, nothing else; if you help, just help, don't take over; if you teach, stick to your teaching; if you give encouraging guidance, be careful that you don't get bossy; if you're put in charge, don't manipulate..." —Romans 12:7-8 (The Message.)***

Our church had completed an NCD survey a few months back, and our minimum factor turned out to be *Empowering Leadership*. Now we needed to come up with a plan to develop such leadership within the church. A small group was formed to look at the issue and to suggest some first steps.

At the first meeting were the senior pastor, a staff member, two of the board members, and two influential lay people. Two of the participants were familiar with NCD concepts, two others were aware of them, and the rest were not.

As we began discussing what could be done to remedy a relatively low score in the area of empowering leadership, Mike, the staff member, spoke out:

"I think we should use the strengths the survey showed us we have, to address our weaknesses," he said.

Those of us in the room who were familiar with NCD principles recognized that this was progress. Our strongest score was in Gift-Based Ministry.

We had a good discussion about the nature of leadership, what the Empowering Leadership score represented, the potential causes of that score, and what steps we might take next.

"I have an idea," said Deirdre, a lay person. "Why don't we identify all the people within the church who have scored highly in the spiritual gift of leadership and 'deploy' them into areas of ministry? That is, everyone whose gift has been identified as leadership could be encouraged to become a leader if they aren't one already. So if any area of ministry doesn't have a leadership-gifted person in charge, we could assign to that ministry a leadership-gifted person who hasn't yet been deployed anywhere."

On the face of it, it seemed logical. But Brian, the board member who had done some NCD training, saw a red flag.

"Hold on!" he protested. "We're in danger of abandoning NCD principles here."

He explained that the growth force of *symbiosis* suggested a body of believers be allowed to develop and express their giftedness as each member evaluated their calling against the needs of the local church.

"If we did what you're suggesting we'd short-circuit that process," Brian pointed out. "You can't just move leadership-gifted people around the ministry areas like chess pieces. They are themselves gifts of God to our church. They're not just 'resources' that we utilize to fill a need."

He reminded us that people with leadership gifts needed to be empowered to find their own roles within the church. We needed to be careful not to remove from them the choice implied in "empowerment."

Fortunately, this part of the discussion was not seriously entertained for long and the group proceeded down a more fruitful discussion path.

"Authentic empowerment is the knowing that you are on purpose, doing God's work peacefully and harmoniously." — Wayne Dyer, American motivational speaker, b. 1940.

For reflection/discussion: *"Leaders of growing churches concentrate on empowering others for ministry." What are the strengths of this focus? What are the risks?*

STORY 9 — GERMANY: UNEXPECTED INSPIRATION

"Remember to welcome strangers in your homes. There were some who did that and welcomed angels without knowing it." — Hebrews 13:2 (GNB)

As a lay leader, I like to do my bit for the church where I can. Recently I was telephoned by Philipp, the deacon in charge of pastoral care.

"Would you mind visiting a disabled brother from South Germany who has just moved into our area?" he asked me. "His name's Martin and he's now living in Sauerland."

While agreeing, out of a sense of duty, to make the visit, I groaned inwardly. This was an area where nobody else from our church lived.

I really don't need this, I thought to myself. But having promised Philipp, I made the effort to drive over.

I was unprepared for what I found. The man had been partially paralyzed since birth, and entirely dependent on help from others. On top of that he was nearly deaf. He needed full-time nursing care, consuming resources without being able to give anything back. Who would have the energy to visit this man regularly (a 30 mile trip) or take him to church for worship from time to time? Cases like his required a lot of effort.

When I reached his home I found wheelchair-bound people in the hall. When I asked the way to his room many were not able to speak to me.

The door opened automatically and suddenly I was standing in front of this man, who welcomed me with a grimy smile and intelligent eyes framed behind a pair of thick glasses. He was skilled at using his hands to maneuver his wheelchair into the right position. His table was piled with serious literature, as well as a specially equipped mouth-organ.

'Hi Martin!" I said, and shook his hand as I introduced myself.

Quickly we became acquainted, and to my surprise we were soon engaged in an interesting conversation. My new friend was able to discern theologically complex issues.

Then he grasped his mouth organ.

"Could I play you a tune?" he asked me.

"Yes please!" I said, and he proceeded to play a delightful melody.

I'd rarely heard live music of such a high standard. This man played like a celebrity!

I was awestruck. I had come to give, and to my surprise had received much more. Immediately I was inspired to invite Martin to participate in our church celebrations [*symbiosis*]. For such a cause no distance was too great.

> *"God has a purpose in every pain he brings or allows in our lives. We can be sure that in some way he intends it for our profit and his glory." — Jerry Bridges, author and Bible teacher, former vice-president of Navigators*
>
> ***For reflection/discussion:*** *Who are the "hard work" people in your fellowship whose contribution is yet to be discovered and acknowledged?*

STORY 10 — GERMANY: HOW *THE RACE* BEGAN

"I have fought the good fight, I have finished the race, I have kept the faith." — Paul (2 Timothy 4:7, NKJV)

It all started when a few teenagers from various churches in Thüringen had a vision to create a prayer network, building on a vision of Marcus Splitt. And so "Prayer Inter Net" was established. Every month prayer warriors received a magazine with various encouraging articles and specific prayer requests, for which they paid an annual subscription fee. After an excellent start our network grew into seventy intercessors, and for the first two years it worked quite well.

Then we had a few personnel changes which meant the size of the magazine could not be maintained, and it was reduced to an A3 format. There were also functional issues because contributors did not always respond to our written reminders. Finally, part of the prayer network vision was the specific training of prayer leaders [*multiplication*] but it seemed nobody from the team was available or passionate about doing this.

During this period we discovered, thanks to our experiences from various youth meetings, that enthusiastic teenagers who wanted to follow Jesus wholeheartedly did not receive enough discipleship training. If there was any teaching through magazines it was either shallow or hard to understand. We began to sense God's leading to create a new Christian magazine to disciple this generation.

What was needed became increasingly clear, and we would need to pool our talents to produce this publication. Moreover, in order to complete this new project the old prayer network, which was not working anyway, needed to cease [*fruitfulness*]. The legal framework for the old prayer network could be adapted for our new project, with minor changes.

The idea for the new magazine took root in 1999, and it was clear that more than one person was needed to make it happen. So Marcus visited representatives from various companies and regions of Germany, inviting them to become corporate sponsors and policy advisors [*interdependence*].

Then we did the preliminary work of mailing, faxing and making contacts with the companies that would become the pillars of the project. We agreed on a title for our magazine: *The Race — Run it! Win it!* with the subtitle, *A new learning booklet for the younger generation*.

During this time of preparation we were able to draw on the skills of various individuals from within our editing team. Marcus developed the central concept and put together a leading group of people. As editor-in-chief he also spoke directly to those who would be sponsoring *The Race*, and cultivated their friendship [*symbiosis*]. Various people provided the expertise we needed, and the closeness within our team meant much to us.

That is how, by the end of February 2000, we were able to publish (by the grace of God) the first issue of *The Race*.

It was well received. Thanks to a board of company representatives who were willing to serve as consultants to the editing team we could constantly improve production and minimize mistakes. *The Race* could also be represented at their various company functions.

For the first three years we did not need any income from advertising. Currently we have 750 subscribers and our goal is for *The Race* to develop in such a way as to remain financially independent [*sustainability*]. That's why we're intentionally working to increase the number of subscribers.

> *"We don't accomplish anything in this world alone ... and whatever happens is the result of the whole tapestry of one's life and all the weavings of individual threads from one to another that creates something.' — Sandra Day O'Connor, US Supreme Court Justice, b. 1930.*
>
> ***For reflection/discussion:*** *What project might you undertake on behalf of your church if you were assured of a team of supporters?*

STORY 11 — GERMANY: ECUMENICAL UNITY

"I am convinced that [in this century] people all over the world will not listen if we have the right doctrine, the right polity, but are not exhibiting community." (Francis A. Schaeffer, ***The Church at the End of the 20th Century.****)*

A few years ago various churches in the town of Fulda took part in an evangelistic week called ProChrist. The common ministry and the good mutual experiences that came out of it were an inspiration to us all. During our shared proclamation of Jesus Christ we were enriched by loving relationships and by taking part in the lives of the others. We recognized how much we needed one another and how we could complement each other. All the leaders from the various Christian churches and fellowships in Fulda have grown closer to one another. At the same time we have appreciated our denominational distinctives and enjoyed our diversity.

Since the summer of 2000 we have met bimonthly with various churches or fellowships for an ecumenical prayer breakfast [*interdependence*]. There we have sought God's presence through united prayer, and have received guidance from his word. We've shared our victories with the other leaders and been brought closer together. Through intercessory prayer we've experienced encouragement and strength for ministry within our churches, and have been able to speak openly with one another during mealtimes, in an atmosphere of mutual understanding.

We've gained new perspectives on spiritual growth as we have worked together in prayer breakfasts, prayers for the city, bimonthly ecumenical celebrations, services in the castle garden, a week of prayer, the ProChrist initiative, a pastoral exchange, and dialog through interviews and discussion panels

In spring 2003 our churches also formulated a common mission, vision and values.

"Build for your team a feeling of oneness, of dependence on one another and of strength to be derived by unity." — Vince Lombardi, American football coach, 1913-1970

For reflection/discussion: The church can cause a society to face God by providing an example of true community. Is there a step you can take this year to foster greater unity among the churches in your city?

STORY 12 — GERMANY: COOPERATING IN YOUTH MINISTRY

*"The goal of a bridge-building leader is to become an effective advocate for each constituent group, ultimately uniting and focusing the efforts of all the groups in such a way that it creates a win-win situation for everyone involved." — Bill Hybels (**Courageous Leadership**.)*

I pastor an independent church in Essen. In 2002 the elders of the Evangelical Alliance in our city wrote me a letter.

"We would like you," they said, "to develop youth work among all the Essen churches."

My first thought was to invite all the youth leaders for a meeting. I wasn't sure, however, how such a suggestion would be received, because I knew what it was like in youth work. All the youth leaders I knew were heavily pressured by their responsibilities and not likely to be interested in extra meetings.

On the other hand we did have several people in Essen who had worked interdenominationally on evangelical youth projects, and I felt I could count on them to come at least once. At first even these people were not interested in another meeting, but because the gathering was interdenominational they made the effort to attend.

"Welcome to this first meeting!" I said to them. "My purpose in bringing you here is that we might clarify how the elders from the evangelical alliance can support you in your work." [*energy transformation*]

The meeting turned out to be very constructive, releasing fresh energy for interdenominational work. They agreed to come back.

At the second meeting we realized that the work of the interdenominational youth ministries was dependent on the youth work run by churches if it was to bear long-lasting fruit for God's kingdom. So we decided to invite to our third meeting the leaders from all the known youth groups in Essen [*interdependence*].

We felt a certain tension at first because many of the people didn't know each other or what good could come from getting together. But the atmosphere soon warmed.

I asked each leader to introduce himself or herself to the group, and gave these youth group reps an opportunity to report on their strong and weak areas.

At the next meeting we sifted out many ideas for more intensive interdenominational work with youth and we created four working groups for various areas -creating vision, city-wide youth worship, mission activities, and internet communication. Each youth leader was invited to join a group that best suited his or her interest and gifting [*fruitfulness*].

It soon became clear that the different groups could pair up for certain projects — for example internet and mission, or mission and youth worship [*symbiosis*].

As the leaders were about to go into their different groups for discussion, I asked them to think about ways they could complement each other.

So this new, open working structure was set up for multiplication from the start.

It became clear that each youth group had strength in a particular area. Some were strong in evangelism, while others excelled in technical support or organization.

"Your individual strengths could be more useful," I pointed out, "if they were to serve not just the local church, or to merely recruit new co-workers. They could bless thousands if they were harnessed for interdenominational work." [*sustainability*]

It seemed a light bulb went on! Understanding this reality has released much creativity and enthusiasm, and the momentum for cooperation among the youth workers is growing.

"Where there is unity there is always victory." — Publius Syrus, Roman author, 1st century B.C.

For reflection/discussion: Are there ways the ministry in which you are involved could benefit by cooperating with similar ministries in other churches?

STORY 13 — CZECH REPUBLIC: HELPING PEOPLE TO FIND THEIR NICHE

There is a place in the body for every member to use his or her gifts. This church enabled one of its members to shine in a new area of creative service — and everyone was blessed.

At our church we want to help all the members use their individual gifts to spread the gospel. We believe every individual has been gifted to serve others in some way.

There are many areas where church members can get involved: children's ministry, social work, cross-cultural evangelism, music, technical support (sound technology), organizing the worship services, home group leadership, mothers' groups, pastoral work, visiting... all of them need workers.

But despite all these opportunities, it sometimes happens that a few people have nothing to do. It's not that they don't want to serve; it's just that there seems to be no area available where they can use their gifts.

Our church sees this situation as a challenge, and if possible we try to create space for a new ministry. The only condition is that the new activity must not be done in isolation but must be part of the church life [*interdependence*]. Church leaders seek to coordinate all ministries, making them complementary and mutually supportive.

A young man called Karel, for example, was converted and joined the church. He worked at an assembly line in a car factory. It was monotonous, unchallenging work, but in the church he appeared to be very creative. In fact he positively crackled with energy and ideas.

When we needed somebody to make the notice-board for the

outside wall of the church, this young man applied himself zealously to the task. He cut out pictures, put them together, wrote short mission challenges and installed little lamps on the board. These now shine at night and attract the attention of passers by.

This activity could not consume all of Karel's energy, however. He was a restless person who jumped during the praise and worship time, shouted comments during the services, and sparkled with wit. He was extremely active, waving flags in church, trying to dance, and conducting the choir.

Once he returned from a conference inspired by short dramas [*energy transformation*] and urged the church to make room for creative skits during the service.

Not all of the members were impressed by this suggestion, however, and some of the conservative ones felt it would reduce the dignity of the worship.

The pastor and church elders debated the matter.

"Should we try to shut Karel down?" one of them asked.

"I reckon!" another responded. "His behavior is getting beyond a joke."

"Before we do anything let's pray about it," a wise elder suggested.

After praying the group felt they should give this new form of worship a chance. And so they encouraged Karel to form a drama and dance group.

Karel gathered together a small group of teenagers and they started rehearsing various skits. They have since presented these during church events, street evangelism projects, youth conferences and at other opportunities.

Ten months later we realize our worship services have been revived and enriched. Members like the short plays and look forward to them. Some of the teenagers have found a new opportunity for self-expression and have learned how to praise God through dancing and drama. The skits are also suitable as sermon illustrations.

One day I planned to preach about the second coming of Jesus. In the morning when I saw Karel in the church, full of his usual energy, I thought about one of their short plays in which the actors stood in line, waiting for a bus. The bus was delayed, and when it finally arrived only one of the passengers had a valid ticket. Karel gathered the group for some quick instructions, and in the middle of my sermon they presented the skit [*symbiosis*].

Karel's gift of organizing and conducting little plays supports the sermon and helps God's word to reach hearts. The listeners might forget the sermon but they will remember the skit.

> *Church leaders recognized and identified the special gifts of this brother, and created space for his unique ministry. Today his talents support the pastor in his own ministry, assist the youth work and enhance evangelistic activities.*
>
> **For reflection/discussion:** *Think of a young person in your fellowship whose energy you could help direct into fruitful service for the whole body.*

STORY 14 — USA: THINKING BIOTICALLY

> ***"But you be watchful in all things, endure afflictions, do the work of an evangelist, fulfill your ministry." — Paul's command to Timothy, 2 Timothy 4:5 (KJV)***

Our church was addressing its minimum factor: Need-Oriented Evangelism. To help us, we scheduled a servant evangelism training event for the next February. Our trainer was a pastor who had employed servant evangelism since he began at his church. It was difficult to schedule the training because of his busy ministry, but we finally settled on a date. Two weeks later we found out that a community event (a large parade) was being held on the same weekend. Not only that, but our largest children's ministry was marching in that parade. (We always tried to practice *interdependence* in our scheduling, but somehow we had overlooked this one.)

So we had a choice: either we could reschedule the training once again, or we could work biotically. We decided to employ the growth force of *symbiosis* by doing a servant evangelism project at the parade. The people at the parade would benefit by our service and we would benefit by hands-on experience.

> *"Out of clutter, find simplicity. From discord, find harmony. In the middle of difficulty lies opportunity." — Albert Einstein (1879-1955), mathematical physicist*
>
> ***For reflection/discussion:** Current secular management literature refers to the principle of symbiosis as "win-win relationships." In other words decisions are made in such a way that everybody wins. As a conflict-solving technique, this is similar to "The Golden Rule." What current problem in your church could you apply it to?*

Growth Force Analysis of this story:

This church was facing organizational challenges. Even though much effort went into synchronizing schedules, there was always the possibility of an organizational bottleneck. Applying the principle of symbiosis in fact started with this perception — which we can only read between the lines in stories like this. Isn`t it great how the solution they arrived at was the result of symbiotic thinking? If we have an appreciation *of symbiosis* — that is, if we value and encourage variety in forms, ministries, styles and methods — we are more likely to see it happening. We overcome not only organizational bottlenecks (as in this story) but also a competitive mentality, the opposite of symbiosis.

When we apply the principle of symbiosis, ministries which have different goals and purposes can be integrated for a common goal. The quality characteristics of Natural Church Development ensure the ministries of a church have a healthy common purpose. Here it is "need-oriented evangelism." Neither the children's program nor the training for this kind of evangelism had to compromise this goal.

Many see symbiosis as simply a way to cobble different ministries together. But this is to misunderstand it, since many of these arrangements lack a well-defined purpose and end up being a compromise nobody is really happy with. Sometimes there is even a tendency to press everybody into the same mold, thus devaluing the specific purpose of each ministry. This is not what true symbiosis is about. But NCD combines both: defining the common goals (the quality characteristic) while at the same time valuing the specific form, style and approach of each ministry, such as the children's program and the servant evangelism training team.

Such symbiotic thinking opens the door for growth force momentum.

We can also see the principle of *energy transformation* at work in this story — for the parade is seen as an opportunity rather than an obstacle. Once the parties thought of a symbiotic solution, they could use their energy to reach a common goal (training for evangelism). We don`t know how the story ended or what the results were (*fruitfulness*), but we can be sure of two things: a variety of ministries were encouraged through this challenge, and the energy of both groups was used to attain the common goal of developing need-oriented evangelism.

GROWTH FORCE 6:

FRUITFULNESS

Fruit is important to God: "He cuts off every branch in me that bears no fruit, while every branch that does bear fruit he prunes so that it will be even more fruitful." (John 15:2) This principle is about defining what "fruit" means before you even start a ministry, and about evaluating on a regular basis everything you do in ministry. Any measure or program that does not bear fruit must be changed or dropped, and everything that does bear fruit must be improved so there will be even more fruit in the future.

STORY 1 — AUSTRALIA: EFFECTIVE WORSHIP

"A good way to evaluate whether our ministry is really in harmony with the principles of church development is to periodically examine our visible fruit." — Christian Schwarz, in Natural Church Development.

In an effort to make our corporate worship services increasingly inspiring, we treat nothing as "sacred cows." Each element usually associated with corporate worship has been tested against a simple yardstick:

"Does this increase the inspiration of the service?"

As a result we have experimented with various components of the service [*fruitfulness*]. For example:

- The location of the musicians (at the front, at the side, at the back, in another room);
- The existence of the musicians (we have also used CDs, tapes, and had unaccompanied singing);
- The location of the worship leader and singers (at the front, at the side, as part of the congregation);
- The way we collect the offering (people bring gifts to the baskets, or the bags are passed around);
- The timing of the ministry of the Word (at the beginning of the service, at the end, in the middle, several times throughout, not at all, or as a small lecture followed by discussion in small groups);
- The timing of the corporate worship service;
- The location of seats within the facility;
- Integration and involvement of children in the service.

If doing something in a new way hindered us from connecting with God, we returned to the old way. If the innovation helped us to connect with God better, we rejoiced. If it made little difference, we felt free to use the new form as and when appropriate.

> *"If worship is mindless, it is meaningless. You must engage your mind." — Rick Warren,* ***The Purpose Driven Life****.*
>
> ***For reflection/discussion:*** *In what ways might the worship in your church be made more meaningful to a greater number of people?*

STORY 2 — CANADA: NURTURING SEEDS

"We should not attempt to 'manufacture' church growth, but rather release the biotic potential which God has put into every church." — Christian Schwarz, ***Natural Church Development.***

Eight years ago I faced a panel of interviewers who were in the process of choosing a pastor for St. Paul's Anglican Church in Leduc, Alberta. One of the members leaned forward.

"What exactly would your agenda be," he said earnestly, "if you became our pastor?"

I reflected a moment. Then came my honest reply:

"I have no agenda except to maintain the status quo."

After all, this was a typical Anglican parish which saw the pastor as answerable to them for whatever happened. It was the kind of church I had been raised in and my attitude came as no surprise to them.

On my first day as the parish priest I knelt before the altar and said, "Lord, this isn't my church, it's yours. Please do whatever you need to do, and help me to stay out of your way."

God proceeded to take me at my word. Shortly afterwards I learned that pastors are responsible to God for their congregation; they are accountable to their members only secondarily. That radical shift ultimately led to an upheaval which culminated, two years ago, in the loss of nearly twenty members.

In 1999 a set of videos had come into my hands from a fellow Anglican priest, which he claimed had made some difference in his own parish. It was called *Natural Church Development* and featured a young German who was vigorously addressing a conference of church leaders.

When I showed it to our church board, it met with resistance from a few members but two or three were intrigued. Throughout the following year, as we dealt with severe conflict within the parish and took to heart the maxim "Conflict is inevitable; combat is optional," new board members replaced those who had departed. During our annual workshop I tentatively suggested we view this same video which had been gathering dust on the shelf [*fruitfulness*].

Their reaction was startling. As the video reached its conclusion and I prepared to tuck it back on its shelf, the quietest member of the board raised his hand.

"Well," he said, "now what do we do? Where do we go from here?"

There was a unanimous decision to move forward, and I was caught off-guard by their insistence. It sent me scrambling to learn more about Natural Church Development. Because the loss of church members had left the parish in dire financial straits, it was obvious we could not afford to arrange for a coach to take us through the various steps. However, my educational fund just happened to have enough money for me to take both levels of training to become a coach — initially to guide the congregation through its first steps. We purchased the survey and managed to find thirty willing participants.

The results were not surprising in an Anglican setting: passionate spirituality was our lowest quality characteristic. Our highest characteristic was not surprising either — loving relationships. The conflict which had reduced our ranks had also increased our strong sense of commitment to the core group that remained.

As we began to work with the results of this survey we made some surprising discoveries. We could readily see not only the interconnectedness of the characteristics within our congregation, but that the seeds of Natural Church Development had already been planted. God had already been working to strengthen our foundation, and we were discovering what we already knew and had begun to initiate-the movement toward small groups, changes in our worship service, and a definition of volunteer positions. We also sensed we would soon be ready to draw up a mission statement and goals that accurately reflected the experience of the congregation's steady growth — as individuals and as a group — in relationship with Jesus Christ.

A transformation was taking place: the knowledge of God was no longer confined to people's heads; hearts were being changed as they began to discover first-hand what an experience of Christ was like.

What began as a casual introduction has become a vibrant life force in the parish of St Paul's, Leduc, Alberta.

"Church growth doesn't depend upon what we do, but upon our recognizing obstacles to what God wants to do." This pastor has these words on a placard in his office.

For reflection/discussion: What would it take to begin a spiritual revolution in my church?

STORY 3 — NORWAY: DISCERNING PURPOSE

"I would give all the wealth of the world, and all the deeds of all the heroes, for one true vision." — Henry David Thoreau (1817-62), American essayist

In the United Methodist Church in Sarpsborg we place a high value on the principle of interdependence. As a result we have become aware of:

- how the soul of the church is expressed in the things we do
- how particular activities affect the whole system
- how the activities of one area of the church affect other areas of it.

We created a leadership team comprised of representatives from all the departments of the church, who would have an overview of the organization. Their task was to evaluate and coordinate the various activities.

We also started to develop a broad goal for the church — a process in which we sought input from as many people as possible, over the course of a year. This resulted in a vision statement that many people could own, and it made decision-making easier. We now had a statement of purpose by which we could evaluate all our activities. This made it easier to set priorities: to decide what we would and would not do. We were seeing the principle of *fruitfulness* at work.

Vision looks inward and becomes duty. Vision looks outward and becomes aspiration. Vision looks upward and becomes faith. — Stephen S. Wise (1874-1949), Jewish rabbi

For reflection/discussion: *Does your church have a vision statement? If not, how could you go about producing one with the maximum involvement of the members?*

STORY 4 — LATVIA: A MINISTRY OF ENCOURAGEMENT

"So then, as often as we have the chance, we should do good to everyone, and especially to those who belong to our family in the faith." — Paul, Galatians 6:10 (GNB)

Once a week we put on a breakfast at our church. This has enabled us to meet a basic need [*fruitfulness*], and as we have met this basic need we have realized we were also meeting other needs: the need for fellowship, relationship and self-confidence, not to mention spiritual guidance. We have informed those who come about other church activities they could take part in, for example Bible studies and Sunday meetings where members of the church participate according to their gifts.

When anyone comes to the Sunday meeting, equipping leadership ensures that person gets the opportunity to minister. As a result many people no longer come to the church breakfast, but they do come on Sundays to receive spiritual sustenance. Loving relationships and powerful meetings are what attract and nourish them.

"Treasure your relationships, not your possessions." — Anthony D'Angelo

For reflection/discussion: *In what ways does your church nourish both body and spirit?*

STORY 5 — NORWAY: CHOOSING A BETTER WAY

"It is always safe to assume, not that the old way is wrong, but that there may be a better way." — Henry F. Harrower

I pastor a 108-year-old Adventist church called Open Door which was replanted two years ago.

One of the challenges of renewing a church is dealing with the tendency to revert to past mindsets, and with the folk who yearn for the old ways of doing things. There happens to be quite a number of old people, as well as young ones, in our congregation. Fortunately the core group understands the need to stay future-focused, and so our church continues to move forward for the sake of the kingdom of God.

An example of *fruitfulness* can be found in the Bible study we do every Sabbath (a tradition in the Adventist church.) The problem in our old church was that the Bible study was not interactive. It was more like a classroom situation, where people would trot out their theological hobby horses rather than share personal stories. The seating arrangement didn't help matters — since the members sat in pews they were always staring at the back of other people's necks. Not surprisingly, some of the young people were beginning to drop out.

"I just found it all so boring!" said sixteen-year-old Janne.

Thus negative energy was gaining momentum.

When we moved to our new location we decided to change things.

"How can we attract more people to our Bible Study?" I asked the group as we gathered together on that first Sabbath.

"For a start we could sit in a circle," said Rolf.

"I think if we shared prayer needs at the beginning and actually prayed for one another it would make a huge difference," added Johanna.

So we did both these things. We always study in a circle now [*fruitfulness*] and the whole session is bathed in prayer beforehand. This has changed the dynamic of our Bible study, which is now far more interactive.

We've also made two people responsible for the Bible study, not just one. The first leads the welcome and prayer part, and the second leads the actual study.

Now the Bible study is self-sustaining, and as pastor I do not need to pour all my energy into it.

"...New wine must be poured into fresh wineskins!" — Jesus (Luke 5:38 GNB)

For reflection/discussion: *What would it take to make the Bible studies at your church the highlight of the week?*

STORY 6 — NORWAY: WHEN THE VISION FADES

"It is the direction and not the magnitude which is to be taken into consideration." — Thomas Paine (1737-1809), English-born American writer and political pamphleteer

Our church had run a program for many years in the little village chapel. The program was always the same: singing, devotions, a raffle and a meal. As time went on fewer and fewer came and the average age of those attending climbed upward. Yet a small group of people continued to appreciate the event.

As the years passed it became increasingly difficult to get volunteers for the various tasks. The same few people were doing all the work, and they were just plain tired. Soon it was just the pastor and his wife who were doing everything, and they got tired too.

At that point the church board began to wonder whether this event was serving any purpose.

Today this little church is no more. It is only a building. Those in leadership understood too late that they should have changed the way they ran these meetings [*fruitfulness*].

"The very essence of leadership is that you have to have a vision." — Fr Theodore Hesburgh (b. 1917), former president, Notre Dame University, USA

For reflection/discussion: "When we always do what we've always done, we always get what we've always got." Does this apply to any aspect of your ministry?

STORY 7 — GERMANY: THE POWER OF GRACE

"For it is by God's grace that you have been saved through faith. It is not the result of your own efforts, but God's gift, so that no one can boast about it." — Ephesians 2:8-9 (GNB)

I pastor a free charismatic church in a small city (60,000 inhabitants) in south Germany. Thanks to some positive but also painful processes, we were able to change, modify and develop our views on building and leading the church.

A few years ago we had the task of developing a leadership team. I focused on building leaders with as many gifts as possible, but did not take into consideration people's backgrounds (home or church) and the dynamics they might bring from these.

We soon had major problems with one person, Mr. P, who by his views challenged not only me and the board but also a large section of the congregation. This person was very legalistic in his views, as revealed in his preaching and conversation. He was always telling people what they as Christians ought not to be doing. These detailed injunctions, often repeated, made many members of our church nervous. In fact, for many, their joy in the Lord began to dissipate.

I had hoped Mr. P's behavior would change and that it had simply arisen out of a difficult time of transition. So I didn't feel, at the beginning, to confront him about what I considered to be his unhealthy attitude [*interdependence missing*]. But in the end Mr. P left the church, taking several member families with him [*negative multiplication*].

At a leaders' meeting soon afterwards we discussed what we should do next.

"We must prevent harmful attitudes like this arising again," said Alexander, a wise, older man who chaired the elders' board.

He glanced in my direction. "Lukas, we need to take advantage of this current interest in law and grace? Why don't you preach a series of sermons on the topic?" [*fruitfulness*].

I agreed to do so, and thus we used the previous problem with Mr. P to achieve a positive outcome.

In any new situation where there was a whiff of legalism we took a firm position based on a clear, grace-filled gospel message [*energy transformation*].

Throughout this time when I, as a pastor, got together with other leaders we were able to discern legalistic tendencies in our own behavior and conversations. So I was very aware of how much we ourselves needed to learn. But now we had an opportunity to start afresh, in a way that would benefit the whole church. It began with the leaders but spread naturally into our pastoral conversations, preaching and other communications [*interdependence*].

As time went on we sensed within the church a new level of trust developing between leaders and co-workers. As leaders we provided new opportunities within ministries and we allowed those who were learning to make mistakes. But any problems were usually short-lived because we gently guided and helped the new co-workers. We worked hard at building trust within the church, and noticed that as we leaders treated one another more kindly, others were inspired to do likewise. When somebody made a mistake we did not get upset; in developing new areas of ministry we focused more on relationship than achievement.

"In the area of pastoral care and other communications it is clear people want a balanced view of law and grace," I wrote in my annual report at the end of that year. "Furthermore, they want a church fellowship in which they are treated as loved family members."

In the end we learned a lot from the departure of Mr. P. We have learned that God can turn things around [*energy transformation*]. We have also consciously moved the culture of the church from being an achievement-oriented congregation to being a family-style fellowship in which new co-workers respect each other and grant one another space. And in the last six years our numbers have almost tripled.

"Give to us clear vision that we may know where to stand and what to stand for." — Peter Marshall (1902-1949), chaplain to the U.S. Senate.

For reflection/discussion: *If you had been this pastor, how would you have dealt with the difficult member when the problem first arose?*

STORY 8 — RUSSIA: MAKING THE MAIN THING THE MAIN THING

"The key is not to prioritize what's on your schedule, but to schedule your priorities." — Stephen R. Covey, American management expert.

Two years ago our church made some drastic changes. Our leadership team had done an assessment of the church and uncovered major problems. Various ministries were not being effective spiritually, and the people coming to church did not have meaningful relationships with one another. The services on Sundays were seldom inspiring, and so people were not motivated to bring their friends along.

Then the leadership team made a decision which to some people seemed entirely negative. We decided to stop all the extra activities that were happening and focus on meeting together on Sundays as the Sunday school and the adult church.

Over the last two years we have continued to feel the effects of that radical decision. Although it seemed harsh to stop certain ministries, it actually brought us freedom — freedom, first of all, to focus on what it means to be a church, and secondly, to restart ministries with new emphases — and sometimes new leaders [*fruitfulness*].

So how do we look, two years on? Well, we have a growing attendance on Sundays as new people are coming to our church and being made to feel welcome. We have started some social and evangelistic work, the youth are meeting together, and people are being saved through evangelistic Bible studies.

Of course many areas still need to be worked on so that more people will be brought into God's kingdom through our church. But we can look back over the last two years and thank God for the way he has blessed us. And we can look forward with confidence to the future.

"Be concerned above everything else with the kingdom of God and with what he requires of you, and he will provide you with all these other things." — Jesus (Matthew 6:33 GNB)

For reflection/discussion: *Is it time for your church to re-assess some of its own ministries?*

STORY 9 — LATVIA: HEEDING GOOD COUNSEL

"Obey your leaders and follow their orders. They watch over your souls without resting, since they must give to God an account of their service." Hebrews 13:17

When I started to lead the church in Daugavpils, I looked for people for the leadership team. Some people had come from other churches and that made it easy (so I thought) as these people wouldn't need any training. I was so grateful!

"You could be inviting trouble," my supervisor warned me. "I'd advise you to teach them anyway."

Unfortunately I didn't follow his counsel.

Later my disobedience resulted in all kinds of strife, as a few of the leaders tried to persuade me to do things the way they had done them in their previous churches. The tension grew so bad that I eventually had to say thank you and goodbye to some of them [*fruitfulness*].

"Get all the advice you can, and you will succeed; without it you will fail." — Proverbs 15:22 (GNB)

For reflection/discussion: How might this situation have turned out differently?

STORY 10 — USA: ROUND PEGS FOR ROUND HOLES

When someone is not happy in his role, it's possible he hasn't found the place where God has prepared him to serve. Leaders and managers often need divine wisdom to help people find their niche.

We had a staff member we shall call Brian, who was a great "fit" for our church culture, but who was becoming increasingly dissatisfied with his particular ministry role. Under the old way of looking at things we would probably have sent Brian off to look for another place to serve. But when we started to think biotically, we began to look at the resources God had provided and to figure out ways to use them in building Christ's kingdom. In this case, the principle of *fruitfulness* forced us to consider the most useful way to employ Brian's unique gifts. We came to see that our small city had a largely unreached people group that he was passionate to evangelize.

By thinking *interdependently*, we were able to forecast the impact of moving Brian to the new ministry and we could replace him with someone who was gifted and passionate to serve in the area he had been serving in [*interdependence, fruitfulness*]. We can also expect the principle of *multiplication* to come into play as Brian helps us to reach the new people group.

"God's gifts put man's best dreams to shame." — Elizabeth Barrett Browning (1806-1861), English poet and political thinker.

For reflection/discussion: Are there Christians you know whose talents could be more creatively utilized for the benefit of their church?

STORY 11 — FINLAND: HOW BIG IS YOUR FRYING PAN?

"You can have brilliant ideas, but if you can't get them across, your ideas won't get you anywhere." — Lee Iacocca (b. 1924), former head of Chrysler Corporation

Over the years I have occasionally needed to question whether what I'm doing (or what we as a church are doing) is taking us where we want to go. That question has changed my way of looking at things — I've re-examined ways of doing even those things that have worked well in the past [*fruitfulness*].

In former times, for example, we used to reach many people through tent meetings, but after a while we realized that the only people who were still listening to the gospel message and enjoying it were the Christians. Somehow we had to find a way to communicate with the secular people of our city.

When some young musicians became Christians we encouraged them to make modern music to a professional standard, with the message of life. And all at once the doors opened. Secular managers invited our group to play in different places, and suddenly we had the opportunity to share the gospel with hundreds of non-Christians.

Another example: Our people had disappointing results when they tried to share the gospel through tracts. Passers-by just did not want to take them, and our church members were starting to feel disheartened.

Then we hit on a different strategy. We invited non-Christian friends to play volleyball with us in the summertime. All of our church members became friends with the visitors, and little by little they started coming to our meetings.

Fruitfulness is the issue. If you don't reach people by doing things in the same old way, why not change?

Korean pastor Cho tells the story of a fisherman who always used to measure the fish he caught with a stick. If his fish was longer than his stick he threw it away, but he kept the smaller fishes. Other fishermen, wondering why he didn't keep the bigger fish, finally asked him outright.

"Before I leave home," he replied, "I measure my frying pan with this stick. The bigger fish just don't fit in the pan."

How big is your frying pan?

"A moment's insight is sometimes worth a life's experience." — Oliver Wendell Holmes (1809-94), American author

For reflection/discussion: *Does your church have an effective strategy for outreach? If not, how could you communicate more effectively with the non-churched people in your area?*

STORY 12 — AUSTRALIA: KEEPING THE CHURCH INFORMED

"First of all, then, I urge that petitions, prayers, requests and thanksgivings be offered to God for all people." (1 Timothy 2:1, GNB)

The person whose task it was to communicate with our intercessor team was finding the task more and more of a burden. So how could we lift our communication to a new level?

Our Gift-Based Ministry coach came up with a good idea.

"Communication might be a lot more efficient," he suggested, "if you produced a multi-purpose document."

So we established a newsletter with the working title *Live*. Its main purpose was still to provide prayer points for the intercessor team. But it would also:

- Focus on a number of quality characteristics;
- Highlight activities and ministries of the church;
- Identify contact persons for those in need;
- Provide a forum for teaching on life issues;
- Allow a broad message from the church leader to be sent;
- Celebrate persons who were on the journey in growing towards the likeness of Christ; and
- Provide opportunity to respond to some of the issues raised in the paper.

Thus one document could have multiple outcomes, as all of its articles promoted the development and growth of a healthy church.

Given our limited resources, this document has become an efficient, effective, God-honoring way of communicating various issues within the life of our faith community [*fruitfulness*].

> *"The prayer of a good person has a powerful effect." James 5:16b*
>
> ***For reflection/discussion:*** *How well does your church's leadership team communicate prayer needs to the church members?*

STORY 13 — USA: COMMUNICATING EFFECTIVELY

> ***"If people can't see what God is doing, they stumble all over themselves; but when they attend to what he reveals, they are most blessed." — Solomon, Proverbs 29:18 (The Message)***

In my present ministry I was leading a seminar on the growth forces, and when we came to the principle of *fruitfulness* we decided to practice it there and then. We began to talk about the things in the church that were meeting or failing to meet their intended purpose.

During the conversation our church newsletter became the center of the discussion.

"What exactly is the newsletter for?" Irene asked. "With its list of events it seems to me just a second version of our calendar."

"That was not its intended purpose," said Alan, who had been a member for many years. "As I recall, the newsletter was meant to minister to our people through articles and stories which were supposed to encourage us."

"Well, nobody's contributed to it for months," remarked Shirley, the office secretary. "Yet I'm still spending hours each week typing it up and printing it out. Since we all get the calendar as well, I'm not sure why I'm still doing this."

"Why don't we just drop it," someone else suggested, "until we can come up with a better format?"

At that there was an audible gasp.

Clearly there were some who didn't like the idea of losing the newsletter. After all, it had been a fixture for many years. But when confronted with the fact that it was no longer serving its purpose they acknowledged the reality — that tasks which were not producing their intended result must be either changed or eliminated [*fruitfulness*].

So we took the brave step of axing the newsletter. The upshot of this is that Shirley's time has been freed up to do more productive things for the church.

> *"There is nothing so useless as doing efficiently that which should not be done at all." — Peter F. Drucker (b. 1909), Austrian-born American management consultant*
>
> **For reflection/discussion:** *Is each ministry in your church achieving its intended purpose?*

Growth Force Analysis of this story:

Before the newsletter was eliminated, three important things happened in this story:

1. Someone had the courage to evaluate — which is a prerequisite for the growth force *fruitfulness*. Evaluation causes us to ask ourselves what ministries are needed for the purposes we have agreed upon. In fact the principle of fruitfulness sees purposes and goals as valuable in themselves.

   In NCD we are encouraged to name the fruit we want. If we have no stated goals and purposes, there is no real possibility for correction, for we don't know why and when and how we need to change.

2. No one was available to take over the original function of the newsletter.

3. Even after the newsletter was seen to be unfruitful, there was opposition to abolishing it. You can be sure of opposition when

> you decide to eliminate tasks which are not producing their intended result. This might be in the form of delay tactics. For example, someone might suggest you need to obtain more information, to verify the ineffectiveness. But doing such research could waste time and energy, especially if the initial criteria were poorly recorded. So the principle of fruitfulness starts at the beginning of each process. (In NCD we call it "planning and testing the fruit.") We record our intended outcomes and start evaluating these early, so we can decide whether any correction is needed. We do this at the same time as we assess our other growth forces. In the long run we'll save ourselves much time and energy when we eventually have to decide whether to persevere with a course of action or to ditch it on the grounds of unfruitfulness.

This story reminds us that it is better to get rid of a program that doesn`t bear fruit than to preserve it. The courage of the person who "tested the fruit" of the newsletter made it possible to see the advantages of eliminating it. The secretary gained more time and space for her necessary work, and renewed energy for the tasks which needed more concentration.

Appendix

- Your Own Story
- Checklist for the growth forces
- The NCD Portal on the Internet
- About the Authors
- Acknowledgements

YOUR OWN STORY

This book is not yet finished. Your story is still missing! Please encourage others by submitting your own experiences with the growth forces to NCD International, and we will make your story available to churches working with Natural Church Development all over the world.

Please use this e-mail address to send us your story: *story@ncdnet.org*

CHECKLIST FOR THE GROWTH FORCES

- Which growth forces do you discover in the story?
- How well have they been implemented? Use the checklist below.
- How could they be improved?

- How could other growth forces be used here?
- What about the balance between the growth forces? Is a principle implemented in a way that contradicts another principle?

Interdependence

- Will it have long-term positive effects?
- Will other areas of church life also be positively impacted?
- Is this an isolated measure?
- Is something here being pushed through without consideration for long-term consequences?

Multiplication

- Will it increase production capacity?
- Has the possibility of multiplication been consciously built in?
- Is the basis for this step the concern about a slow beginning?
- Is the motto "Addition rather than no growth at all"?

Energy Transformation

- Have the needs and gifts of those participating been recognized?
- Is resistance dealt with constructively?
- Has there been an appeal to people's guilt?
- Is resistance countered with appropriate counter force?

Sustainability

- Does the intended goal have a positive impact on the original situation?
- Does the measure support itself?
- Is this measure a one-way measure?
- Is it necessary to invest more energy because the measure fails to "kill two birds with one stone"?

Symbiosis

- Do team members, activities, etc. complement each other?
- Does this measure encourage variety in forms, styles, methods, etc.?
- Is there a tendency to press everybody into the same mold?

- Is there a feeling of competition between different workers, departments, etc.?

Fruitfulness

- Does this measure integrate clear criteria for measuring success?
- Has it been decided how and when the success of this step will be evaluated?
- Are motives other than church development driving this step?
- Are "sacred cows" preserved rather than slaughtered?

THE NCD PORTAL ON THE INTERNET

Visit the NCD Portal site at *www.ncdnet.org* to find:

- More stories how churches applied the growth forces
- A free NCD online magazine ("eNCDine")
- NCD Online Training
- Free downloads
- The latest NCD resources
- Links to other NCD websites

ABOUT THE AUTHORS

Christoph Schalk directs the Partnership and Consulting Network of NCD International. In addition, he serves as the scientific and statistical director of the Institute for NCD International. He studied psychology and theology in Würzburg, Germany. Christoph has written several books on NCD, among them a *Pastor's Guide* and a *Mentor's Guide* for gift-based ministry. He also co-authored the *Implementation Guide to NCD* that has been published in more than 20 languages. For many years, he was the

Chief Editor of "Praxis," the magazine of the German Church Growth Association. He is an international trainer, speaker and coach, having conducted seminars in more than 25 countries.

Julie Belding, MA, BTheol, is a New Zealander and the current editor of *DayStar*, a monthly evangelical newsmagazine. She was formerly the editor of *The New Zealand Baptist* newspaper and has edited several books. Julie and her husband Russell, who develops software, have lived in Auckland for 19 years and attend a Baptist church. The Beldings have two adult children and two young granddaughters. Julie's hobby is playing Internet Scrabble

Daniel Catalano, MA Phil. Intercultural Studies, is a trainer, speaker and coach on the topics of "interdependent thinking," "how to implement feedback," and "team development," in churches and schools as well as being a management consultant at *A & O Consulting*. In his training he gets to the heart of issues and people by using both analytical methods and practical, powerful illustrations. Daniel's mission is to develop training topics that create the best parameters for personal effective paradigm shifts. He and his wife Miriam, who studied psychology, have lived in Würzburg for seven years and attend a charismatic church. Daniel delights in traveling and making music.

ACKNOWLEDGEMENTS

First of all, I want to thank all the people who have contributed to this book by sharing their stories: pastors, leaders, members of churches on all continents. Without you, this book would be like a box without content.

I also want to thank my co-authors Julie Belding and Daniel Catalano.

Most of the story-tellers who wrote for this book are not native English speakers, and neither am I. Julie helped all of us to be better in English, and came up with helpful insights in her comments and reflection questions.

Daniel used his analytical giftedness to bring all the stories into a system, and did the in-depth analysis for this book.

Thanks also to Thomas Fode and Petr Cincala for their work on our "story database" and all the feedback during the development of this book.

Finally, I want to thank my wife Annette for reviewing the book and shaping its concept … in order to see more fruit.

Christoph Schalk